The Quest for Staff Leadership

Geoffrey M. Bellman

Scott, Foresman and Company
Glenview, Illinois London

86491

ISBN 0-673-18194-4

Printer's key—1 2 3 4 5 6-RRC-90 89 88 87 86 85

Library of Congress Cataloging-in-Publication Data

Bellman, Geoffrey M. 1938-
    The quest for staff leadership.

    Bibliography: p.
    1. Management. 2. Leadership. 3. Line and staff organization. I. Title.
HD31.B3785   1986   658.4'02   85-19603
ISBN 0-673-18194-4

A BARD PRODUCTIONS BOOK
Editing: Alison Tartt
Cover Design/Production: Mark Kohler/Suzanne Pustejovsky
Text Design: Mary Ann Noretto
Text Illustrations/Script: Mark Kohler
Composition/Production: The Composing Stick, Austin, Texas

To Sheila

Contents

Working with Management

Serving Customers

Supervising Staff Professionals

Managing Your Career

Conclusion

Preface

There are more of us working as staff, service, or support function managers in organizations than ever before, literally millions. Despite our large numbers, few management theorists or practioners have written books about us. We get a chapter here and there in general management texts, but seldom a book. We deserve and need much more attention than management literature is currently giving us. Many of us are searching for special staff guidance.

Managers of personnel and purchasing, data processing and law, accounting and government relations—all staff departments—have much more in common than they ever talk about. That is the first premise of this book. The second premise is that effective staff managers lead from behind—in step and only one step behind, but behind nevertheless. Learning to lead from this support position is essential for exceptional staff managers. The third premise is that an individual must integrate excellent managerial performance with clear personal direction to be an outstanding staff leader. Every chapter springs from these three points.

I had two intentions as I wrote this book. First, I wanted to search out, for myself, what makes a staff manager especially effective—that is what "the quest" is about. Second, I wanted to give voice to my experience in a way that other staff managers would find useful. The first intention was fulfilled after two drafts; it took three more drafts before I was satisfied that I had completed my second intention.

Fourteen years as a professional, a supervisor, a manager, and a leader in three corporations provide a major source for the contents of this book. Another source was working with and watching staff managers during the last seven years as a consultant. I have worked with staff (and line) managers in more than one hundred organizations, consulting to some of them for five years. The third source is more personal: I have spent two-thirds of my life engaged in work of one form or another. While working, I have struggled with and enjoyed discovering relationships between my work and my life's meaning.

Those three sources flow together into a book that is strong on opinion based on experience. Its message is clearly my message; its style is conversational and controversial, not academic or objective. Others have benefitted from these ideas, and I believe many of you can, too.

Geoff Bellman

Introduction

Welcome to the Quest

1

I am a staff manager, not a line manager. Those of you who have been there know there *is* a difference. Your experience has shown you how different it is to manage a support or service function. Your experience tells you this though the literature does not. What you read is aimed at the line manager and feels a bit off target for you, the staff manager. It is useful—but does not quite talk from your experience.

My quest for staff leadership

Along with many other staff managers, I struggled through wondering what my job was and how I should do it. Where could I go for guidance on this unique role? My best guidance came from successful staff managers who had a few years of experience and wisdom to put behind the guidance they gave me. Some especially perceptive line executives helped, but most of them did not understand enough to both help me learn and empathize with me along the way. Line executives seldom dealt with the difference in an equal and positive fashion.

Too often I found the staff differences from the line being acknowledged in negative and superior ways: "You staff people . . ." Or "It's hard to understand if you aren't on the firing line." Or "When we want staff input on this, we'll ask." See what I mean? The difference is recognized, and the recognition is not complimentary.

When I went to other staff managers, the reviews on who we are and what we do were mixed. Many of them were buying into the words expressed to me by line executives: "How much can you really accomplish if you only have a staff job?" Or "I don't like it, but what can I do about it from this position?" Or "Look, I do what the line tells me to do and I try to do it well . . . Isn't that enough?" So again, the differences are seen as negative—and also rather inevitable.

There was also a rather passionate and vocal minority of both line and staff managers who held out for a more ideal staff management role. They had experienced staff managers and their departments behaving in new ways, ways outside the assumptions behind others' statements. They saw staff functions as important in determining company strategic directions, as having a clear sense of staff purpose, as initiating projects with the line management, as dealing with line executives as equals, as being worth including and listening to, as having power in the organization . . . Now, *these* were the people I enjoyed talking to! Their visions of the possible staff future paralleled my own thoughts and experience.

Somewhere in the midst of all this exploring, I decided to write about it, whatever "it" was. With time, I discovered that I was searching for those special qualities that make staff managers both strong in their functional area and influential in the larger organization. And I discovered that strength and influence could not be had by simply managing the staff department well. In fact, you can be one hell of a department manager *and* quite weak and uninfluential in your organization.

What is needed is leadership—staff leadership. And that requires quite a different set of abilities than a manager necessarily displays. And it is quite different from what everyone but the vocal minority saw as being possible for heads of staff departments. Leadership involves vision, discipline, power, passion, and followers, among other things. No one could say these are descriptors we ordinarily apply to staff managers, but it is possible to apply them to some of us some of the time.

So this book is about leading from a staff management position. It describes thoughts and behaviors that will help you think about and become the kind of staff leader you want to be. It asks many questions and gives some answers, but seldom in a prescriptive way. Because it does not lay out a path so much as lay down a challenge, it really is in the nature of a quest. We are searching for examples of staff leadership together, knowing we will never find the absolute best way. No one is going to publish the basic rules and procedures for staff leadership. Instead, staff managers like you and me are going to continue searching for better ways of leading.

During this quest for staff leadership, we maintain faith that through persistent application of our abilities, our staff department can become what we envision. At the same time, we know that the realities of our organizations and ourselves will often frustrate the accomplishment of what we want. Balancing the vision and the reality yields a practical idealism that accepts the organizational world while working to improve it. That is what the quest and this book are about. Join me for the next thirty-four chapters as I search for staff leadership. Along the way you will get some glimpses of what staff leadership is—or can be. Perhaps you will learn about how your work can serve what you want out of your life. Perhaps you will pick up a few new ways of approaching your job. In any case, you will learn more about a perspective on staff leadership that is risky and rewarding, empowering and ennobling.

For those who can say, or would like to say:

"I contribute much to my organization's effectiveness now and have much more to give."

Is this book for you?

"I give a significant part of my life to this work because it is a valuable way to invest myself."

"I gain great personal satisfaction from the work I do."

"I am dedicated to pursuing excellence in my work."

"I have chosen my position and see it as a primary means of making some contribution to this world."

If you support these idealistic intentions about your work in a staff department, then this book is for you, i.e., you've already been searching and are ready for the quest in earnest. If you no longer share those ideals; if you are not curious about how a staff management position can offer that kind of meaning, then you probably ought to pass the book on to someone else. The book is about the quest for life meaning through your work.

The book is written for the staff manager who:

- Has unique responsibility for a staff function in the organization.

- Has expertise that is almost entirely confined to this function.

- Has two or more professional people reporting to him.

- Has a budget.

- Has access to upper management.

- Has objectives, reconsidered at least annually. Somebody expects something to be delivered from this staff function.

- Has been in this work more than two years.

That describes the reader I have in mind. You may meet only half these criteria and still find the book useful.

This book assumes experience in the staff management role. It is written for those staff managers who have been around long enough to develop a basic approach to their work. They are no longer asking questions about what the job is or what management is or what is expected of them. They have some answers to these questions—and are constantly improving on those answers. They have faced the trial of dealing with a difficult line customer; they have won and lost influence with top management; they have struggled with the competent and unmotivated employees; they have succeeded; they have failed; they have been there.

They are not looking for prescriptions, for the step-by-step solution. They know (or at least suspect) that this kind of "truth" doesn't exist. What they really need is a few kind words from peers who have faced situations similar to theirs and have survived. Maybe even thrived! They are looking for ideas that they can add to their experience and convert to visions, thoughts, feelings, and actions.

How to read this book

Though some of you will read this book cover to cover, my intent was to appeal to those of you who are more likely to read a piece at a time. You will notice in thumbing through the book that it is made up of a number of shorter topic areas grouped into chapters and sections.

Though there is logic to the book's design, that logic is not as compelling as the individual topics it contains. Do not hesitate to open it to a random topic and start reading. That could take you to another topic on either side of the one just read. Most of the topics make sense on their own. A few are quite long, usually those containing a list or a process or occasionally a sermon.

Like other recent writers, I struggled with pronouns that recognize both male and female readers. I chose to alternate between "he" and "she" throughout the book, striving for an equality here that society has yet to achieve.

The book is conversational and informal rather than academic and comprehensive. It provides thought for you to fit within your conceptual framework; these are not prescriptions. The book asks you to think about your work and what your work has to do with living. It reinforces some of what you now do and take pride in. And it asks you to consider alternatives to the way you are managing and leading now.

Possible outcomes from reading this book

No guarantees, but this book does give guidance toward a number of possible outcomes, including:

- A better understanding of the possibilities and rewards of being a staff manager.

- New perspectives on what you are doing and could do in your job.

- Improved self-knowledge about your willingness to take risks.

- Increased clarity about your independence/dependence needs in carrying out your job.

- Tactics for dealing with your boss.

- Ways of influencing the organization to help it give you what you want.

- Increased confidence in and comfort with how you approach your job.

- Knowledge about how effective you are with your employees.

- Skill tips to help you be more successful with your organizational customers.

- Thoughtful consideration of what you want from your career and its importance in your life.

- A departmental strategy endorsed by your top management.

- A systematic way of managing your department supported by your employees.

- A list of departmental project priorities for this fiscal year.

- Verifiably improved relationships with important customers.

- A career development and personal growth plan.

- Testimony from line managers about the effectiveness of your department. (You must be kidding!)

- Evidence of line organization change that would not have taken place without your department's assistance.

- A performance discussion with your boss.

- Inclusion of your function in key management policies, systems, procedures, or rules respected and honored by the line management.

This book helps you consider your career in staff management and the rest of your life. I intend to bring additional meaning to the work in your life. The book will not likely get you a promotion, a raise, or even a pat on the back. I contend that going after any of these things disempowers you since you do not control them. Do not turn them down when they come along, just don't make them a primary objective. You do not control them, and they can control you. Promotions, praises, and pats are controlled by others; wanting them puts you in the hands of those who control these external rewards. For you, that can mean trouble.

The rewards of acting on what you read

Do not expect the organization to congratulate you for wise management when you develop an idea from this book and it works. Don't even expect them to understand. Other things are more important to them. If you get the external recognition, well and good, but do not make it the reason for your being.

If you take any actions as a result of this reading, do it for yourself—for your growth and satisfaction. Starting now, begin to align your performance with the results that indicate quality staff management has been accomplished. Your reward will be primarily internal, subjective, impossible to quantify, and much greater than others can bestow. This is what makes the quest worthwhile.

Being A Staff Manager and Leader

✔ **Overview**

✔ **Leadership: A Staff Perspective**

✔ **Staff: What Are We?**

✔ **Meaningful Staff Management**

✔ **Variations on Your Role**

Overview

Since this is a book about staff leadership, let's consider what leadership is in this context, particularly how it differs from management. The first chapter in this part of the book differentiates leadership from management. The second chapter sorts staff from line. Rather than developing fine definitions, these two chapters describe leadership and staff through examples and elaboration. The last two chapters in this part of the book have to do with what the staff management/leadership role is, and what it can be. We need to explore various ways we can approach our role. All four chapters are intended to stir your thinking about what kind of a staff manager and leader you are—and want to be.

No matter how you cut it, staff management (and leadership) in today's organizations is tough! Whether you are director of public affairs, vice-president of human resources, manager of purchasing, or supervisor of graphic arts, your work is cut out for you:

- You deal in a world that worships line functions and that thinks, acts, and talks in terms of "the bottom line" or "the end product." And bottom line you're not.

- Your most important customers (or users or clients) are people who do not understand what your function is about—and often do not care to learn.

- To make things even harder, the users of your services see you as less important, subordinate, ancillary, overhead—cost centers to be at best tolerated and at worst abused or eliminated.

- There's also a good chance you are living with a departmental reputation that dates back to your predecessor's.

- And let's not forget your neighboring staff departments, troubled by turf issues, jealous of their domains, and seeing you as competition for organizational resources and top management favor.

- And, just in case this is not enough, there is your staff, ranging from those dedicated to reaching a comfortable retirement to those who want to seize control of the corporation in the name of accounting systems, personnel, auditing, or drafting, or whatever function you manage.

Exaggerated? Certainly, for many . . . True? For some . . . False? Not completely. Chances are those six points contained something of you in them. You would have said it differently; you would have emphasized one point or added another, but, as a staff manager, I doubt you would totally disagree. You are reading this book, and that itself is one clue to your needs.

The six above points are about a world that many staff managers live in and must cope with. When they—and you and I—search for professional meaning, it is in such a confusing and rubble-filled world. I propose that living in such a world can be professionally wonderful.

This book is about the "wonder" of staff leadership and the choices it offers you in the quest for meaning in your work life. It is about altered perspectives on your work (like the last statement in the previous paragraph). It is about doing the professional managerial job you can take pride in.

Leadership: A Staff Perspective 2

Yes, there is a decided difference. And that difference is important to why this book is titled *The Quest for Staff Leadership* rather than *The Quest for Staff Management*. The direction to increased staff effectiveness and satisfaction is primarily a leadership direction rather than a management direction. In fact, it was tempting to speak of us all as "staff leaders" rather than "managers" throughout the book, but it sounded awkward. When you see the words "staff manager," realize it includes both roles. More and more writing supports the differences between management and leadership, so let's elaborate on them.

Management and leadership

Management

- Decisions made in relation to established directions.
- Emphasis on logic and structure, supported by intuition.
- Concern with using resources effectively.

Leadership

- Decisions made in relation to a vision of the future.
- Emphasis on intuition, supported by reason.
- Concern with expanding resources.

- Performance measured against plan.
- People working within plans and schedules.

- Commitment to your assigned responsibility.

- Analytical, logical, sequential, objective.
- Practical, concrete, and present-oriented.

- Performance measured against possibilities.
- People working according to what the project requires now.
- Commitment to the larger project, doing whatever is needed.
- Subjective, intuitive, organic, creative.
- Impractical, conceptual, and future-oriented.

These columns represent extremes for the sake of definition. In fact, the leadership/management distinction is much more difficult to make since behaviors come from people with mixed needs, intentions, abilities, and situations. Individuals trying to sort out where they are on a continuum will need an instrument much more precise than these columns.

And, at least in their extremes, management and leadership are different. They represent different perspectives on the organizational world—what is important in it and how to behave within it. The perspectives are within each of us, and we vary a lot on where we are on the management/leadership continuum.

As the left-hand column indicates, management has to do with the plans you write, the procedures you establish, the objectives you pursue, the more concrete evidence you have of what you intend to do, how you intend to do it, and how you are doing along the way. Management makes sense. It is important, and we will talk more about it.

Read the right-hand column again, and you will find that leadership does not make sense—at least it is not based in sense. Leadership has to do with the vision, the intuition, and the risk possible in your job. It is the gut-level decision you make before all the data is in. It is the impromptu talk you give to your group about the kind of department this could be. It is the gutsy stance you take with management based on your strong professional values. Leadership sets you apart. It is based on belief in yourself, in your people, in your function, and in your ability to achieve something more. It requires an expression of confidence and commitment that goes beyond what the data tells you is justified. Leaders look at today in relation to the vision they have about what tomorrow could be. They make decisions today that will move them toward that tomorrow.

Running a department well requires skills in both leadership and management, the emphasis varying with your situation. Most of us come preprogrammed to be better at one side of the job or the other. We need to assess our skills and see how they fit with our situation. My emphasis here is not upon what your management and leadership skills are but rather to legitimize with you the existence and interplay of these skills and perspectives. Recognizing the need to pay attention to both can affect how you deal with situations. For example, it will tell you that you need to appeal to more than reason when dealing with your subordinates. It will tell you that having a dream of what this department could be is terrific and not enough. It will tell you to pay attention to those hunches of yours that run counter to what reason dictates. It will tell you that you need to attend to the heads and hearts of yourself and the people you work with.

The next comments elaborate further on leadership from many perspectives, removed from the complications of daily organizational reality. I express what leadership is in this way to allow you to compare how you and I think about leadership, as well as to encourage you to think about yourself as a leader. Notice which parts are particularly appealing or unappealing to you. Ask yourself how you lead, how you want to lead.

Perspectives on leadership

Leadership is not primarily a rational process. It can build on a rational base with planning, organizing, and controlling, but these are aids in the exercise of leadership rather than its essence. Management is not leadership and a good leader is not necessarily a good manager. Leadership has more to do with visualizing

Leadership and vision

what *could* be than sorting out what *is*. It has to do with acting in relation to that vision, if not articulating it for others to embrace. It means making decisions in relation to that envisioned future rather than in relation to the pressures of the present.

Leadership and commitment

Leadership is characterized by commitment to a vision. Passionate commitment. The clarity of what could be combines with the awareness of the resources now available to help the leader get there, to convince and motivate the followers to do what must be done today to move us toward tomorrow. Whether the leader is a general in the army or a staff department manager, they share in this ability to speak to their followers in ways that cause the followers to want to contribute to realizing the leader's dream. The ways they "speak" are not always with words; often actions alone suffice. The "dream" may be as large as a world at peace or as small as making this a fun place to work, but the followers believe in it, believe in the leader's ability to move them toward it, believe in their own ability to contribute to bringing the dream into reality.

The leader's commitment precedes and builds the commitment of the followers. Her commitment shows in all that she does. She has an obvious clarity about how what is happening in this moment relates to where we are going together. Her commitment usually exceeds that of all but her most devoted followers. She frequently makes demands on others that they do not believe they can meet— and they perform at levels far exceeding what they thought they were capable of. Their self-esteem almost always increases in the process.

Leadership and energy

Dreams are not realized through small investments of energy, and leaders portray this. They give more energy to the cause they are leading and cause others to give more. And not just an extra 5 percent. The quantity and quality of energy given is orders of magnitude beyond what is released under uninspired leadership. One perspective on leadership is that it is the building and releasing of energy directed at an important goal.

Leadership and risk

Leaders create and take risks. They step out beyond the boundaries that their followers were living within. They do so on the strength of their belief in what could be. They see the world differently because they look at it through their image of what it can become. Then they risk taking steps toward that imagined world. That imagined, dreamed of, envisioned world is their primary frame of reference for all they do.

Taking risks means making decisions. Leaders make decisions in relation to their vision. Managers make decisions in relation to preestablished policy, objectives, or directions. Leaders establish directions by making decisions.

Taking risks means making decisions that do not make sense, in the narrower meaning of that word. Leaders decide because their intuition, heart, or gut tells them what to do. This is not a rational decision-making process with carefully weighed alternatives and all the risks quantified with all the information needed readily available. Leaders usually decide long before their more scientific associates have even collected all the data needed for a decision.

The leader's style of getting things done varies greatly and is not a critical element of leadership. You can find leaders all along the spectrum from autocratic to democratic, and each can work given the supporting task, situation, and followers. Vision, commitment, energy, and risk are all essential to leadership; a particular style is not.

It is easy to argue that an autocratic leader will be less successful in today's corporate world than one who is more participative. Though this will often be true, having a participative style is not as essential to being a leader as having a vision of what could exist, as being heavily committed to that vision, as bringing great energy to realizing that vision, as having followers.

Leadership and style

The label "staff manager" is apropos of what most of us do. Apart from our personal inclinations, most organizations expect us to act more congruent with management than leadership. Many line executives would cringe at the thought of their

Staff manager or staff leader?

staff managers becoming leaders. And I think we staff managers do not lead enough—that is the major premise of this book.

If we do anything well as staff managers, it is manage—and we do too much of that and not enough leading. Leading from a staff position is no easy task. It requires much more flexibility and finesse than when you have the authority of the line behind you.

Our lack of leadership models among staff managers is one of the primary reasons we lack leadership abilities. Not only do our line managers not expect it of us, we seldom expect it of ourselves. Few staff managers truly lead, so there are few footsteps we can follow.

What if things are not going well in your staff department? Will that discomfort cause you to want to change things, and will that stimulate you to lead if you are not now leading? Discomfort provides a willingness to act, but doesn't tell us the direction to move in. We need more than discomfort. We need models; we need skills; we need confidence; we need alternatives to what we are now doing.

Staff leadership and action

What are alternatives for staff managers wanting to demonstrate leadership? Read quickly through the twenty items listed below and you will get a sense of what you can do to lead. Then go through the list slowly, circling those actions that might be adapted to your situation, checking those that you are already doing, and crossing out those that you wouldn't consider in your organization:

1. Write a "white paper" on the future of your department as you envision it. Picture the contribution you would like to be making to the company and articulate it in print. Emphasize the parts that would be especially exciting for you.

2. Involve your management team in describing a common vision of what this department's unique contribution could

be. Perhaps instead of or maybe in addition to no. 1, unite your team through discussion of and agreement to the larger purposes of your staff function. Again, build on the exciting themes that come out in your discussion.

3. Tell your management the directions your function ought to be moving in—but only after asking them for their input. Find a way of speaking to the top management about what you envision for this organization and the ways your department can support the larger organization's directions. Use this opportunity to both educate them and get their support.

4. Encourage innovation within your unit by making sure that there is always at least one new project or possibility being researched.

5. Expect creativity of each of your direct subordinates through building it into their objectives for the year.

6. Ask your entire department to assess you as a leader. Find out both what you are doing well and where you need to improve. You may choose to do this with a meeting, a questionnaire, or through a series of interviews using a consultant.

7. Ask your boss to assess your leadership behavior. First discuss what leadership is together—perhaps both of you could read this book or an article on the subject. Then tell your boss how you assess your leadership. And follow that with your boss's assessment of you.

8. Isolate one leadership behavior you believe you need to develop further and publicly commit to doing it differently.

9. At your next staff meeting include an agenda item that asks everyone to brainstorm solutions to one of the department's nagging problems—and resist the need to come to final resolution of the problem today. Instead, just generate the ideas and let them incubate for later action.

10. Talk with each of your key professionals about why they work for this company in this staff department. Try to get a sense of how their presence here ties in with the larger purposes in their lives. Also see how their motivation relates to your own.

11. Tell key individuals on your team about why you work here, what's in it for you, and how your job here is important in your life.

12. Hold a dinner for your staff that has no purpose other than to tell them what a wonderful job they have been doing contributing to the department's directions. Give a short but intentionally inspirational talk about the importance of what they are doing. Give it from the heart, revealing how important this is to you.

13. In a one-on-one meeting with a subordinate, encourage her to give her greatest effort to the work, tell her that this is important to you, and promise to recognize her efforts.

14. Greet change in the larger organization with enthusiasm, looking for opportunities to apply it to your function. Be the first to embrace efforts aimed at making the company more effective.

15. Initiate a productivity improvement effort in your department that begins with the improvement ideas of the workers and brings these ideas to your attention. Reward successfully implemented ideas.

16. What was the last important idea that you took to management that didn't get accepted? Find another way to take it back to them that will more likely gain acceptance.

17. Involve your staff in coming up with ways to develop themselves.

18. Establish performance criteria within the department that

assess the individual against leadership indicators like independence, risk-taking, commitment, innovation, etc. Add these to your present discussion of performance against objectives.

19. Bring together managers from related staff departments to explore new approaches to an old and common problem. Lead this process.

20. With your staff, isolate the line department you are having most trouble being effective with, and develop an approach that requires you to behave differently toward them than you have in the past.

Though brought together here in a condensed list, you will find many of these same ideas explored in greater depth in other parts of the book. The list emphasizes thinking far ahead, seizing the initiative, being the first to risk, dealing with others in a less hierarchical manner, expressing enthusiasm, and articulating your vision. That is what staff leadership is about.

Staff: What Are We? 3

Staff, service, support, support function, specialist, functional specialist—these are all words I have heard applied to the people I wrote this book for. They can be characterized as outside the core line activities and dependent on those activities for their existence.

What is "staff"?

What are the line activities? I think of production and sales as the core elements of a simple manufacturing organization. Finance and marketing are often included as line functions when they demonstrate a direct contribution to the bottom line. These are the people and processes and equipment through which the primary work moves to reach the objectives of the organization. All of us who are outside this primary path of work and authority are, to my notion, "staff": public relations, traffic, research, purchasing, personnel, auditing, accounting, security, maintenance, affirmative action, engineering, drafting, safety, medical, mail room, reproduction, administrative services, cafeteria, public affairs, labor relations, human resources, data processing, information services, and a host of others, all staff.

Staff vs. line

- You do not have the final say; you recommend and pray.

- You manage a group of experts or specialists more loyal to their profession than the organization.

- You manage a function nobody else understands.

- You have access to a wide range of managers in the organization.

- You have lots of ability and relatively little positional power.

- You get to deal with powerful people more often than many people in the line hierarchy do, though the issue is usually not as important as line matters.

- Your contribution is difficult to measure.

- Your upward growth in the organization is limited to your functional area.

- You suffer from regular accusations of not understanding or appreciating "the big picture" or "the bottom line."

Putting staff and line at the ends of a continuum is a way of understanding the difference:

Staff ←	→ Line
indirect	direct
think	do
advise	decide
supportive	responsible
expert authority	position authority
specialist	generalist
prepare	perform
service	product
cost center	profit center
contribution	results

Although this approach polarizes the two beyond accuracy, it gives us a feel for the important differences.

Staff work is defined primarily by its relationship to the organization's purposes. It is a dependent relationship characterized by statements like:

- "In the end, bottom-line responsibility for the company's success rests with Sales, not with me."

- "My satisfaction comes from helping Manufacturing get their work done more effectively."

- "I make input to the production manager so she can make better decisions."

- We measure our effectiveness by how well we meet the EVP's needs."

- "I advise Finance; they decide what to do. They measure me on how well my advice works."

Stability vs. change*

Operations groups are rewarded for stability. They are searching for the best way, and when they find it, they don't want to let go of it. Staff groups, on the other hand, are rewarded for making improvements, for changing things for the better — especially high-level staff groups in planning, public affairs, human resources, and management information systems.

So a conflict is built in. The line organizations can easily move to a defensive position. And we can easily push them there. From this position, they feel compelled to hold on to what they have been doing, because to let go of it would be to acknowledge that we know better and/or that they have been doing it wrong for all these years.

* Based on the ideas of Barry Leskin.

That is just what so often happens when either of us does not do our job well. When they see a staff person coming in the direction of their department, their inclination is to batten down for the storm. We screw things up by implying that they are not that smart, that we know better, that we already know they are screwed up and it is just a matter of time before we find out how.

Line: output-focussed*

Line functions have always had a multitude of measures on what they do. Their product is critical to the company's success. This importance requires ever more precise and immediate measures of results and, in turn, individual and departmental contributions to those results. There is no denying the importance of making sales, of pushing a product out the door, of meeting quotas, or of making deadlines when these are tied to company and individual performance.

This output-focussed system and mentality is compelling for many managers who are a part of it. They live, rise, and fall by the numbers. They love the clarity of the results (some of the same appeal as sports) and also have to play within the rules of the game. Saying that meeting this month's quota is no longer important to you is the equivalent of a quarterback saying it no longer matters who wins. The surrounding rules elevate the results in importance. For those who choose to play, the results, the rules, and the game can become all that is important.

The game—be it football or sales, baseball or manufacturing—becomes a primary source of meaning. It gives individual recognition. It holds out goals that others recognize as important. It provides ready and agreed-upon measures of performance. It encourages participants to work with others toward shared goals. It says to those involved, "You are important; you are needed; you are among friends. Here is your chance to do something in life, to make a difference." That is a pretty powerful message.

*Based on the ideas of Marvin Weisbord.

Most staff managers do not get this message that clearly; most staff managers do not play in that game. Yes, we do respond to a message like that, but it is not as meaningful for us as it is for the line manager. Yes, we follow the game closely; we support it as referees, trainers, scouts, team doctors, cheerleaders, water boys, and ticket takers support a football game, but we do not play. We do have games of our own, pressures of our own, needs of our own, meaning of our own. Our meaning and pressures and needs are every bit as important to us as the line players' are to them. It's just that we have chosen positions that depend on the line players for their existence and execution. No backfield? No scouts . . .No team? No ticket office . . . No plant? No personnel office . . . No accounts? No accounts receivable.

The corporate cultures we are a part of honor the output that lets the corporation know how it is doing. And the cultures humor the people who deliver the output; they are the stars of the game. The way we think within the culture, the terminology we use, the rewards and punishments we give are all keyed to the line values. That is just the way the game is played. Trying to change it is as difficult as changing the height of the goal posts. It's not impossible, but it certainly takes a lot of work.

Staff: input-focussed

If line groups are output-focussed, are staff groups input-focussed? To a large extent, yes. Since we find it so difficult to evaluate our contribution, since our outputs are at best only one of many that are used by the line management of our organizations, we fall back on our inputs. We emphasize credentials. We have to believe this is a good report because look who worked on it and at the background they have. Sure, other experts could have come up with other conclusions, but we will choose to believe our experts becaue they are well qualified and we have no objective way of judging their product.

Staff departments are inclined to overbuild their expertise. An oil-industry economist told me that the company really only used his expertise once or twice a year. The rest of the time he did work that required much less expertise than he possessed. For doing the work of a junior economist most of the time he was paid a senior economist's salary all of the time. This was the company's way of buying insurance on their economic decisions—and a good example of loading up on the input if you have no good way of judging the output.

The emphasis on input also leads to specialization—knowing more and more about less and less. As staff managers with some functional expertise, we are aware of how much there is to be known about our particular field. The people working for us are even more aware about our field and less concerned about company needs than we are. Combine this with our desire to be on top of the latest expertise (or at least the need to stay ahead of our own management), add our eternal hope of making a huge contribution to the organization that everyone will recognize as uniquely ours, and you have the recipe for increased staff specialization. In plusher economic times, this is not looked at too closely, but comes the recession and all kinds of obscure staff specialists are walking the streets wondering what happened to them.

Staff managers are responsible for providing some kind of reality check that keeps the overspecialization we are so fond of from happening. The basic check is easy to get from a line manager. Just tell her what each of your professional staff members are working on right now and listen to the questions that come in your direction. The basic question is: "What has *that* got to do with getting the product out the door?" A good question; I hope you have a good answer. A related thought: if you had to rank-order all of the work your department does in terms of what it has to do with getting the product out, what would come first? last? and what's the order in between? Now, how well does everyone who works for you support and understand that rank order?

Clients, users, employers, patients, managers, whatever label you may put on them, these are the people who justify our professional existence. We survive as long as they continue to use us. To that extent our situation is much like the manufacturing plant that must find a market for its product, or the restaurant that needs diners, or the university that needs students. Our world of potential customers is smaller, our dependence is greater and more evident.

No one label covers the gamut of people that staff serves; we use a variety of terminology according to our function and organization. I selected "customer" because I'm growing to like it and because consistency throughout the book is helpful. So when you see the word "customer," know that I am talking about those people (especially) and organizations and systems that you serve. "Customer" causes us to think in terms of our marketplace within the corporation. It helps us define ourselves as a business within the business. Customers buy; we sell. So we'd better think about what we are selling.

"Service" is what we do for our customers. Service does have its nobler side, but carries the obvious implications of "in service to" or "in the service of." This makes the dependence of the staff role all too clear for many of us. We do not like to recognize our limited marketplace or its capability of limiting what we do. Again, there are parallels to the larger world that our corporation lives in. For evidence, think about the last time legislation was threatening to control or reduce the marketplace your company depends on for its existence; remember the reaction of your top management to those potential constraints.

Yes, the corporation has a larger world to work in. Yes, the actions of the corporation are usually not watched as closely as are our staff actions. And yes, the corporation does have reactions similar to our own when the controls on it seem to be getting too tight. As staff managers, we are choosing to live within the boundaries of the corporation. We accept the reality that our resources will be used within the walls of this organization. While this acceptance limits our options (e.g., as accountants, we cannot be the premier accounting firm in this region), it also increases our potential for impact in the smaller world we choose to serve (and we can build the best accounting system this corporation has ever had!).

In return for our commitment to serve, the corporation offers us its resources, a place to work, a paycheck, a position, and a chance to influence directions and results. All of this comes on a regular basis. The reliability of the organization in delivering what we need is important to the reasons we choose to stay inside rather than try to provide the same services in the larger marketplace of the world. Some of us also have talents and needs that require resources that cannot be marshalled by one person on his own; only a large organization can bring together the financing or equipment or technical teams needed to do what we want to do. Others of us find the larger world professionally lonely and choose to serve a corporation because of the companionship it offers. Still others of us like the discipline that the organization brings to us; its structures are easier for us to work within than building our own. And others believe that the only way to get anything really important done in the world is through combining forces with other like-minded people in an organization and making something happen together. Our reasons for staying in organizations are many and important and provide the motivation behind our contribution.

Meaningful Staff Management 4

This closing line from an old joke about the optimistic child looking through the pile of horse manure that he got for his birthday has something to do with what I am talking about. It represents the extreme in altered perspective (though we've seen others knee-deep in organizational waste looking for "ponies"). To be successful and fulfilled in staff management you must feel that it is worth it; there really is hope; progress can be made; this is of value; there is a pony. Without this optimism, forget it. Bringing forth positive energy is not possible over the long term if you work from a base of cynicism or pessimism.

There must be a pony in there somewhere

How many people in your organization have a job like yours? How many people share your job description? Most of us as staff managers have few functional peers in the organization—and that is one of the things that makes our jobs extra hard. If you

Let's face it, we're alone

were a sales manager, or a production supervisor, or a regional operations vice-president, you would have at least a handful of people you could call to talk with about your work. And they would know what you are talking about because they are reaching for similar goals with similar resources within the same overall plan.

When a staff manager looks for consoling, she often has to turn to people with responsibilities quite different from her own. Something is missing. Have you ever noticed how popular staff professional associations are? I think it is because staff people are professionally lonely. They can go to the annual conference, find somebody with a job like theirs, pour out their problems, and get back ideas they can use. That is wonderful! But they have to go outside the company to find somebody who understands. This isn't a complaint; it is an assessment of the reality for many staff people. And the situation is even more acute for managers of staff professionals. This "alone" experience is part of what defines the unique staff management role.

Accepting our role

Here is a list of what we must accept to perform as staff managers and lead reasonably healthy lives:

1. *"I will never be president."* Perhaps of the United States, but not of this corporation. Look at your own organization and the background of its last three presidents. How many of them made it to the top through staff positions? If you have ambitions for that most senior position, you had better get into another line of work—or work of the line.

2. *"To advance upward, I must be willing to move to other companies."* For all of us except those who work for huge, multidivisional corporations or agencies, this is the prevailing truth. Continued advancement is within the profession, not the organization. It seems difficult to make more than three upward moves in one company before coming to a block. Up-

ward mobility is not all that is important, but it is something staff managers pay attention to as we look for ways to contribute to our own growth and the organization's.

The movement of staff managers from one company to another increases suspicion that our loyalties are primarily to ourselves rather than the company. This is, of course, true—as it is for almost everyone. It becomes a problem when those suspecting our loyalty are obviously loyal to this organization; just look at the service stripes on their sleeves. The newer staff manager becomes the new guy who wants to change things and move on.

3. *"I am not in charge here."* I may be in charge of this department, but I am not in charge of this company. I may agree with your ideas, but I am not in charge of policy. I do submit strong recommendations, but I have to live with the decisions of others. Those of us with high needs for control will live in constant frustration because so much that is important is not ours to determine. Many of us have to live with decisions that we do not even get to influence. That is even more frustrating! We can't even say, "Someday, when I'm in charge . . . ," for reasons explored earlier. There are many things we can control in ourselves, in our department, and in our work, but we cannot control important elements of the company. They can control us.

4. *"I will learn a lot about a little—and become known for that."* Specialization is our joy and our sorrow. We develop our talents in a rather narrow realm and take them to a wide population. Our expertise opens many corporate doors for us, but once inside, we are seen as offering little from a large perspective, or lots with little perspective. With this come our labels. "He's only a safety man." "Don't ask her about management, she's a scientist." "He's just a bean counter. What would he know about motivation?" The other side of the label is much more rewarding: "If you ever want to know anything about advertising, ask her." Or "He's our expert on the law; let's listen to him." Or "We'd like your informed input on this before we decide."

5. *"I am a **staff** manager, not a line manager."* Some of us have a hard time accepting that basic truth. I hear myself and others pretending to be more important. I hear us hinting at the power we have from behind the throne. I watch us acting strong with our subordinates and weak with our superiors. This is all related to how we deal with being staff rather than line. For some of us it is status-related. For others it is impact-related. For yet others, it is control-related. And for whatever reason, I hear many of us saying, "Yes, I have a staff job, but I'm really more important that that . . ." Those words sound more apologetic than accepting.

Unique or strange?

"What *do* you people do over there, anyhow?" "Well, you know how they are over in the staff departments." "Does the company pay you for doing this stuff?" Comments like these are how others reveal they have noticed that you are different from them—and not necessarily in ways that they like. A more positive perspective on these apparent put-downs would be to say that they appreciate that there is a difference. Our response is too often to deny that difference or otherwise defend ourselves.

Large organizations are not noted for positively reinforcing differences. Combine a department's "different" responsibilities with the fact that it is a *cost* rather than a *profit* center and you've got a staff department with image problems.

A mistake that many of us make is to say, "Hey, we are no different from the rest of you; we all want the same thing, etc., etc." This attempt to homogenize ourselves is seldom believed, and is generally ineffective. Instead, find positive ways of acknowledging the differences, valuing them, and, through action, showing your special contribution to the organization.

We are unique. That is to be said with pride—and loudly in the right settings (like your own staff meetings). Uniqueness means knowing who you are, being able to sort yourself out from others in the organization. But in an objective and profit-centered organization uniqueness is not enough; it must be coupled with contribution. It is not enough to be special; we must be special contributors.

A meaningful staff management job and the meaning of life are intertwined: to be the excellent staff manager, examine what is important to you in your life and translate those core values into your work. Meaningful work will sustain you at deeper levels.

The meaning is there; find it. I do not say bring meaning or add meaning, but find meaning. Look around and see what you can find that is meaningful to you. If your search for meaning in your life doesn't yield much, look to another part of yourself and build on what is there but hasn't been explored much yet. If your search for meaning in your staff job doesn't yield much, try looking at your job in new ways, explore it from different perspectives. If that doesn't work, move on to a job that holds more meaning for you.

How will you know it when you find meaning in your work? It has something to do with relating what is most important to you in your life with what is most important to you in your work. Work that has meaning provides important linkage between internal personal values and external personal action. Meaningful work is seen as the expression of self through job performance. If the workplace were a stage, you would be an actor, playing yourself. The workplace allows for you to be yourself, to find yourself as you work in it.

Most staff managers make at least a few of these meaning-filled statements:

- "I want to make some small difference in this world, and my work allows me to do that."

- "I prize my family and need to bring my best energies to them. I have a job that I like well enough and do well enough in fifty

Finding the meaning in staff management

hours a week, so I have plenty of attention to give to my home life."

- "I have always wanted to contribute to significant social change in this country. I feel very fortunate to be in a company and a position that takes my efforts, adds them to others, and is attempting to impact the nation."

- "It's a big world and I just want a place in it where a few people around me value what I do and think that I am important. That's what my job does for me."

- "I want to live a life of relative independence, free of financial concerns, with the opportunity to travel and learn about other cultures. I've got a job that lets me come and go as I please. I'm pretty much my own boss. I make a good salary and I like the work. What else could I ask for?"

Notice that each statement speaks to both what is meaningful for the person and how the job supports that. The personal aspects of the meaning are evident. Even if some of the above quotes do not fit with you, you can recognize how they could be very important to someone else. If you were to write a statement about how your life and work meanings are connected, what might it say?

To the extent you can find meaning in your work that is personal and that relates to the basic reasons why you are here on this earth, you can measure your work satisfaction against your internal standards. This allows you to eliminate, reduce, or avoid the tyranny of other people's external standards. You can play the professional staff management game knowing that it has only the amount of importance you have given it. You know that your beliefs, your internal standards, are more important than the priorities of the organization you work for. You have personal success criteria that outweigh all other criteria. This puts you in a powerful position— and requires that you be a powerful person. You maintain the perspective that you are working for this organization because it serves your beliefs and values to do so. Retaining this personal clarity is difficult in the face of so many other tempting perspectives. Core beliefs that result from a conscious exploration of alternatives, carefully chosen and used as guides for daily action, give you power over your work life that many only imagine.

Not the only game in town

This is especially important to staff managers because there is so much in our work that says staff management (and therefore our contribution) is secondary. And within the rules of the corporate game, staff management *is* less important. This is much easier to accept if I know the corporate game is not the only game in town; in fact it is only one of many games that I can choose to play. And I am playing here because it serves me well to do so. It's like I am playing in a much larger game of my own design where the stakes are much higher. That game is called "My Life."

The rules of this game say that:

• I have to decide what is important in my life.

• When I take action that moves me toward what is important in my life, I get points.

• When I take action that moves me away from what is important in my life, I lose points.

• I keep score as I play.

• The game started with my birth and ends with my death.

• There is no way to win, lose, or quit. (I am reminded of a quote from Stan Herman: "You can't win; you can't lose. But you've got to play because it's the only game in town.")

Now that's one helluva game, isn't it? No wonder we opt for corporate games that carry the illusion of total meaning, of winning, of losing. No wonder we rely on others to make the rules and say we will live by them. It is so hard to take responsibility for the whole game—to be player, coach, scorekeeper, and spectator, not to mention rulemaker.

We love the bumps*

All of us who ski have been tempted to leave the smoother, groomed runs for the risk and excitement of the mogul fields—the "bumps." Some of us yield to the temptation so that we can tell stories at the end of the day about how we almost killed ourselves. We love to tell about how hard it was and how much we hurt as a result. A listener might think we had been forced onto those steep, bumpy slopes. But no, we do it on purpose! And we love it!

That perspective on skiing expresses well what I am attempting to say about the staff manager's world. We love the bumps! Most of us would curl up and die without the challenge of the daily problems we deal with. And we love to tell others how hard the "mountains" are that we face and climb and ski down daily. We like to show off our cuts and bruises to appreciative listeners. The "bumps" are a critical element of our work and our measurement of our success.

Our bumps are the special rush projects, the meetings, the critical comments on our work. Could it be we love them all?

Try this on:

"Thank you, Mr. VP, for requesting that project report by nine o'clock tomorrow morning. Thank you, Ms. Project Leader, for setting up that half-day meeting on product development. Thank you, staff, for letting me know that we are slipping behind on the XYZ program. Thank you all, because I *love* the bumps; that's why I'm here; that's my challenge! The interruptions, the hurry-up projects,

*Based on ideas adapted from T. Gallwey and B. Kriegel, *Inner Skiing* (New York: Random House, 1977).

the changes in direction, the tight constraints, and the "bumps" give definition to my efforts, challenge my skills, and make my work life interesting. No bumps? No me!"

Now some of you are saying that life is a little *too* interesting right now. Very possibly. It is possible to kill yourself on the bumps, be they in the Rockies or in the office. I offer this perspective not to suggest that it replace the way you see your world now, but only to bring you another viewpoint that has worked for other staff managers. It does not reduce the workload one bit, but it does ease the stress and reduce the griping about the workload.

Variations on Your Role

5

As staff managers we can perform our role in a variety of ways. Many of us do not stop to look at the alternatives available to us, the immediate reality being so compelling that it apparently blocks our consideration of how else our job might be done. I find it useful to think of a continuum of eight responsibility levels, as shown below:

Staff roles continuum

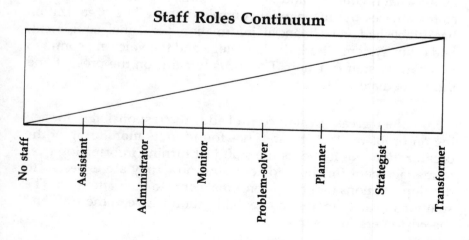

Staff Roles Continuum

No staff · Assistant · Administrator · Monitor · Problem-solver · Planner · Strategist · Transformer

No staff

The extreme left side of this continuum represents an organization without staff departments. The line takes care of all its own needs; each unit is quite independent and self-sustaining—at least in respect to staff functions.

Assistant

Moving a bit to the right—far enough to let staff departments exist—we find line departments making all the decisions and using staff to do the detail work that leads to the decisions. At this point, staff is not making recommendations. They do not have a complete understanding of the project involved; they just do what they are asked to do. The old "gopher" label is appropriate as they "go fer" this and "go fer" that.

Administrator

Here we see the staff continuing in its old data-gathering functions and adding some conceptualizing. The line delegates routine decisions to the staff that have more predictable outcomes and through experience have been shown to distract the line organization from day-to-day operations. This is a more administrative position focussed on support matters needing attention now.

Monitor

Next the staff adds to earlier responsibilities that of monitoring what is happening and has been happening in the organization. Part of the monitoring role is reporting out to the line on how they have been doing. This role brings with it the power of knowledge about what is going on and the responsibility for speaking up. The staff exercises the managerial controls that the line organization has established on its financial, information, personnel, equipment, and other systems. Both the knowlege and the voice are confined to a narrow staff function. The focus remains on the present and the immediate past.

Problem-solver

Now the increase in staff control adds the responsibility for acting on problems that the staff has found in its monitoring of the organization. No longer is the staff just turning information over to management for them to act upon; now they are expected to develop solutions to the problems that come to their attention. The solutions usually require some joint action between the staff and the customers they serve.

The problem-solving focus on the present and past is now turned toward the immediate future. The staff begins to help the line with its planning by thinking about how the line can carry out its functions during the next year: what are the operational considerations that relate to this particular staff function? The line is the initiator of the planning and asks for staff help in thinking the plan through or filling staff gaps. The emphasis is on what management wants to accomplish over the near term and how this staff can help realize that accomplishment. Within the staff group, people are assigned planning responsibilities in addition to the day-to-day problem-solving and systems maintenance responsibilities they have been carrying in the past.

Planner

The staff perspective is extended beyond the operational plans of the next year to the strategic perspective of the next three to five years. At the least the staff is being asked to fill the blanks in the corporate strategic plan—similar to what it did with the operational plan at the last notch. The stronger end of this role is when the staff is asked to do the initial strategic thinking for management and present staff thoughts as a starting point for the line's thinking. Note the potential impact of this position as the staff shapes what it thinks the future will hold and in effect asks the line to think within that framework.

Strategist

This position of greatest staff influence and control transcends what most staff departments are doing and have ever considered doing, and probably my ability to articulate it. The transformer role has to do with staff visions of the future of this organization, the world it is a part of, and the changes that are evolving in both. From this position the staff manager would be thinking of the corporation as a small and important force in a much larger environment and attempting to gain a more holistic perspective on the meaning—and potential meaning—of what the corporation is and does. This involves looking at the organization as being in a state of constantly becoming more, adapting to its surroundings as it affects those surroundings. The manager would be bringing this larger perspective to those who guide the corporation, helping them determine what is important to them, helping them navigate by the stars that they use for guidance, helping them steer toward a future that is unknown and can be influenced.

Transformer

Assessing your role

Your staff probably performs at a number of points on that continuum. Let's consider your real roles through these questions:

1. Is there any pattern to the functions you perform? Are they clustered within one role on the continuum?

2. From a time perspective, what is the orientation of the work your department does: past? present? near future? distant future? far out? You probably noticed that the control level on the continuum increased as the staff department paid more attention to what is going to happen in the future than what has happened in the past.

3. Has there been any movement in the roles you carry out over the last two years? In which direction on the continuum?

4. Where would you like to be on the continuum as contrasted with where you are? How ready are you to make that move? Do you have the abilities you need to manage a department that has more of a future-oriented role than you presently have?

5. Look at the talents of the people working for you. How well are they prepared for where you would like this department to be going in terms of the continuum? What abilities do they need to develop? What abilities do you need to hire?

6. What are the implications of the moves you would like to make on the continuum for the structure of roles and responsibilities within your department? How might it affect what individuals do? How could you start to work on it today?

The continuum moves from a past to a distant-future orientation; it moves from a reactive to a proactive stance; it moves from a task perspective to a world perspective; it moves from a dependent position to an interdependent position with management. As discussed earlier, a staff department will find itself at a number of points on the continuum simultaneously. The challenge is to both know where you are and where you would like to be so you can lead your department.

Roles lend themselves to labels, and labels are often affixed to staff departments. How we are labeled is important to how and whether others use us. Labels stick for a long time and are not easy to change. I have created some generic labels that may relate to the way you are seen in your organization. I draw them from familiar jobs in the community and apply them to their staff counterparts. As you read through these, be thinking about how the label helps or hinders a staff. **Staff labels**

This is the staff group that hands out tickets on other people's authority. The group is known for having responsibility for finding out what is wrong, for catching others at violating the rules. Policemen are out in the organization actively seeking felons. An auditing department that only finds fault is a good example. **Policeman**

Though not out actively seeking offenders like the Policeman, the Judge evaluates all that is put before him and makes decisions about how it fits with the rules. The Judge does have the authority to act, and this action is very difficult to appeal. A public relations department that reviews the contents of all speeches before they are made is acting in the role of Judge. **Judge**

This character is one whose primary responsibility is to help others learn about something that is important to the organization. Staff departments that invest a good deal of time in educating groups or individuals, like the training department or the safety department, fit the Teacher characterization. They stand for the better way, how we want to do things, and are usually disturbed about how we are doing things. **Teacher**

Shopkeeper

This role describes the departments that wait for someone to come through their doors before springing into action. Then they do whatever is asked for promptly and with some deference since "the customer is always right." Support groups like reproduction and word processing often run themselves like a small, self-contained shop.

Bookkeeper

A step farther removed from the action out front, Bookkeeper departments keep track of the numbers. They keep the books up to date and don't worry about what is done with the data they collect. They are not confined to the accounting department by any means. They can be found in any department that has a lot of numbers to crunch.

Craftsperson

Here is the staff person, quite skilled in her trade, who spends hours crafting a project, program, or system to precisely fit the needs of the organization. These people are the bridge between the real world and the more creative types that we'll talk about next. One example is the systems department that helps redesign the company's production and inventory control system.

Egghead

Seen as especially bright and even more impractical, these people and organizations make their way in the company by coming up with the occasional brilliant idea that more than pays for all of their other ideas that didn't work. These are the explorers who hopefully find the company's future while they are searching. An obvious example is the research department. Other examples might be found in the strategic planning and organization development groups.

Operator

These people are just busy; they are always working. They apparently have few concerns beyond what is in front of them. They are focussed on doing their job without thinking a lot about what happens on either side of it. They would be hard to separate from their counterparts in the line organization. A good example would be the people who are on the hardware end of an information services department. They are as production-focussed as an automobile assembly line.

These people move paper. They specialize in forms. They are seen as worshipful of the policy and procedure manual; it is the ultimate authority. They have an especially clear understanding of what their job is—and know that everything else isn't. They are noted for expecting the system to maintain itself if everyone does his part. They are reluctant to step outside the system and respect its pace over the urgency that any individual might express. Government agencies are especially known for their bureaucrats, but corporations are not immune—especially those that deal with the government on matters like taxes, affirmative action, employment, and environmental impact.

Bureaucrat

These are the departments that take care of the spiritual needs of the organization's members. Employee assistance, career development, training, and counselling are all good examples. The label includes a preoccupation with the person's needs to the point of neglecting the organization's. This is where you can go for a friendly and confidential chat without fear of reprisal. This is the corporate confessional without the absolution but with the confidentiality and guidance.

Minister

Some departments are given—or take—the special responsibility of poking at the corporate ego at every opportunity. Their effect seems to give the organization perspective on how great it really is, plus they can stimulate new thoughts and alternatives. Most of all, they risk their existence since carrying out this usually informal responsibility means treading a very narrow line. Doing the job well requires the ear of top management and the respect of top management. Various staff departments can take this role, though it seems to be most often held by those who are expected to do longer-range thinking for the organization—planning or economics, or perhaps the legal department.

Gadfly

In reading through the list, you may have seen a label that others would stick on your staff department. Or perhaps you found one you would apply to yourself. A few comments about the labels and the labelling process:

Perspectives on labels

1. *The label can become the reality*. People are drawn to the simplicity of a label. It means that they no longer have to think about who you are because they have you figured out. Then they are inclined to see those behaviors that fit with the label, with the way they want to see you. This can be true whether we are talking about an individual, a race of people, or a staff department.

2. *Your department has earned the labels it has*. At least look at that real possibility. Perhaps *you* did not participate in the process, but somebody did, and if you want to change the label you are going to have to work against that residue of old feelings that back the old label. Find out what has contributed to others seeing you the way they do. This will give you some clues about how to unstick the label you find on your forehead.

3. *When you get a label, it is hard to escape it*. There is no way to make a frontal attack, and anything that you do about it must be done through time. Your actions will reveal how inaccurate the label is; your words will just draw attention to the label in ways that often reinforce it.

4. *Consider how you want to be seen*. Most of us would like others to appreciate a little more of the complexity of our staff functions—rather than just hanging a label on us and forgetting us. Perhaps if we can just keep others confused but interested, that is enough. Better yet, if we can educate them about some of the finer points of our work and build their appreciation for it at the same time.

5. *Dropping a label means acknowledging being wrong*. This is what you are up against in many people's minds. It is not just that they are compelled to accept your department on new terms from this day forward. No, it is that they have been thinking about you in other less accurate ways for some time, probably spoken about your department to others . . . now they have to change all that. This prospect of change is reason to hold on to the old labels longer. Yes, it is an uphill fight.

6. *Your department is going to be labelled; make sure it's a good one.* If there is an inevitability to people putting stickers on you and what you do, then pay attention to this process and affect it. Think of your services as a product that is in need of marketing. If you were Procter & Gamble, how would you market this product in this organization? How can your customers see what you want them to see?

7. *Be what you say you are.* As a department, behave in ways that obviously fit with how you promote yourself. This is what others will notice most. The image you want to project is just fluff if it is not backed by behavior. Providing excellent staff support is the best marketing tool you have. Help others realize what you are doing and could do. Marketing of yourself is more education than it is advertising. Focus others on what you do rather than sell what you could do.

8. *Changing a label starts with your actions, not theirs.* If you are concerned about how you are seen, then do something about it! Griping about the unfair regard that others hold you in focusses attention on them and does nothing to change the situation. Instead, decide how you would like to be seen and what you could do through your work that would allow your function to be seen that way. Then go out and do it—and don't expect changes overnight. It took a long time for your department to get the label it has and this label is not easily removed.

9. *An inaccurate and widely held label means the organization does not understand.* Truly. Do not dismiss the label. This is valid data about how your department is perceived, and you should pay attention to it if you want to be used effectively.

10. *If you do not help your customers understand what you do, they will make something up.* They are going to have some perception of you just because you work there and they deal with you. Accepting this fact, why not have them think about you and your function in ways that more accurately reflect what you do? You are going to end up dealing with their perception of you anyhow; do it sooner rather than later.

At the risk of overemphasizing the importance of image to the detriment of substance, we must acknowledge that staff departments often do have image problems. The best way to destroy an old and inaccurate image is through work that proves it outdated. And that work needs to be supplemented with effort from the staff manager that educates the organization about what this staff department is now doing.

Managing Toward Results

✔ Overview

✔ Visions and Mission

✔ Values and Philosophy

✔ Goals and Strategy

✔ Objectives and Plans

✔ Systems and Methods

✔ Structure

Overview

The next six chapters present a staff management perspective on visions and mission, values and philosophy, goals and strategy, objectives and plans, systems and methods, and structure. These terms are probably familiar to you, but too often we staff managers withhold consideration of these important elements because of our built-in dependence on line organizations. We have said that we cannot think about our mission until the organization we serve clarifies its mission. Or we cannot plan for the next year until the line tells us what their plans are. In fact, there is a great deal we can do with little or no direction from our management and our customers.

I view these upcoming chapters as elaboration on what management academicians have written on these six areas. See my comments as staff applications of their work. The chapters are connected and proceed hierarchically from the more conceptual and long-term considerations involved in visions, to the more defined and immediate guidance available in methods. Most of us are better acquainted with the more concrete end of this hierarchy; our daily work lives are full of it. The fact that we have spent less time at the top end of the hierarchy does not make it any less important. Actually it is probably more important because we staff managers have neglected it for so long. It is in this top end that we will find new alternatives and strength.

Visions and Mission 6

There is increasing recognition of the relevance of the ideals we hold in our hearts and minds to the reality that faces us at this moment. Chances are you are reading this book looking for ideas that you can use on the job and also that you can relate to some greater ideals that you hold as a staff manager.

It is those larger dreams that bring meaning to what we are doing today, when we can envision the kind of department or job this could be. We feel lost when the reality becomes a daily grind that does not seem to serve our vision. For many of us, the dream is unarticulated but no less real for not having said it. We still know when we are acting in concert with it or in conflict with it.

As an individual and as a staff manager, know what it is you are reaching for. Talk it out with others to find out more about it. Write down your thoughts about what kind of department you want this to be. Dare to reach out beyond the day-to-day reality to express the ways in which you would hope to contribute in this organization. This articulated vision becomes a kind of guiding star that you can see from anywhere on the organizational and professional landscape. In the confusion of daily work it is difficult to

On dreaming the impossible dream

Express the dream!

maintain direction without some kind of guiding vision of the way it could be.

Think ideally; act practically

What are the immediate benefits of all this refined visioning and dreaming? First of all, you will know who you are and what you want as a professional staff manager. This internal guidance system allows you to maintain a larger perspective in your daily work. It is more likely you will be able to sort through the trash and trivia to find what has meaning in relation to your professional vision.

It wasn't many years ago that management readings did not include words like "ideals," or "hopes," or "vision," or "dreams." The emphasis was almost entirely on the practical—application, doing, action. Recent experience has opened our eyes and altered our focus; our new lenses have changed our perspective. Today's manager continues to pay attention to the immediate, practical aspects of getting the job done and does that job within a more ideal framework than ever before. We are making progress.

Why do we exist?

Mission has to do with unique purpose, be it your own, your department's, your company's. A mission statement answers the questions "Why do we exist?" and "What are we in business to do?" and "How are we unique?" Corporate mission statements have been with us for years, but only recently have they been widely recognized as critical in guiding the corporation into its future. On an individual level, life-planning workshops and career development consultants have been promoting the importance of individuals deciding what their life missions are. The corporate and individual consideration bestowed on the term "mission" suggests that staff departments ought to be thinking in terms of mission, too.

There are indications that we are ready. It is becoming increasingly apparent that more of us have a mission of some sort as we move out of the reactive stance of giving higher management everything they want without question. We are moving away from just keeping track of what is going on and toward telling management what they should be paying attention to. Increasingly, we are expected to initiate, to speak up when not spoken to, to tell management where we think they ought to go (where we used to just imagine that opportunity). This evolution of our role points toward clarifying what we are about—our mission.

What might a staff department mission consider and contain? It should be a short paragraph (three or four sentences at most—if it is too long, no one can remember it). It should not only clarify this department's overall, long-term direction but also sort out this department from the others that surround it in the organization. The statement should identify what the department uniquely contributes and how it wants to make this contribution.

The needs of the larger organization, the customers served, should be honored in the mission statement. The link to the company's overall mission should be obvious. And the value of the statement to the staff management should be apparent. That is, in reading it, you should be able to see how it would be useful in helping staff members decide whether their actions supported the mission of the department.

Just reading a staff's mission statement is only getting 30 percent of the message it has to convey. The greater part of the message is in the development of the mission statement. The work on mission brings those involved closer together; they become a team as they develop their mission. It gives them a common purpose and identity that they understand in a unique way because they participated in the conception, gestation, labor, and birth of this new definition of what they are about.

Elements commonly found in mission statements* include:

• The basic product or service offered.

• The primary people being served by the department.

• The technology used in the delivery of the product or service.

*Adapted from J. A. Pierce II, "The Company Mission as a Strategic Tool," *Sloan Management Review*, Spring, 1982, pp.15-24.

- The fundamental concern for survival shown through the emphasis on meeting the needs of the customers in the organization.

- The way the department wants to be seen in the larger organization.

- The way the department sees itself and wants to be seen by its own members.

This is what a mission statement contains. Now, how do you write one?

Creating a mission statement

Focussing on the reasons for our department's existence requires listening to ourselves and listening to the organization. Neither is easy. Sure, we listen to ourselves now, but much of the time we are so busy reacting we don't stop to figure out what we *want* to be when our department grows up. Stepping out of this reactive rut and up into our possible future is a shaky step onto unfamiliar terrain. We frequently don't know how to take it and don't know where we want to go together. And since where we go is affected by this organization we serve, we must also listen to them as well as ourselves.

So how do you do it? The underlying process is rather straightforward.* Collect data from the organization and from yourself and analyze it. Write a mission statement describing the ways in which your staff department wants to serve the larger organization. Follow this with a presentation to management, with their modification and support of your staff directions.

Here are nine ideas useful in talking with others about their directions and expectations of your staff function:

1. Consult the written word. What have they said about where the organization is going and how it is going to get there? Look at the strategic plan (if there is one), read the annual report, get copies of speeches executives have made recently, analyze the operational plan, review the budget, talk with the people in the planning department. Do all this paper

*Chapter 25 presents a consulting process you could use to create your mission.

homework before meeting with a single executive. This reading will prepare you, give you a sense of organizational history, and increase your respect for the importance of history to this organization's survival.

2. Decide which persons you want to talk to in the organization—if you could talk to anybody. Then decide whom you will talk to. As you have less time and resources, narrow your group to those few individuals who could likely tell you more.

3. Talk directly with people; don't develop questionnaires. You need data that is much more alive than a questionnaire can provide. You need the flexibility of an interview.

4. Set up short (30–45 minutes) interviews with people and allow enough time in between to extend the interview if *they* choose.

5. Collect data with another staff department that performs functions related to yours. One risk of what I am recommending is that you will do it—and so will the staff managers in seventeen other departments, thereby beseiging top management with interview requests from staff and managers who don't seem to know what in the hell to do.

6. Prepare useful questions for your interviews such as:

   • Where is the organization going over the next three to five years?

   • What are the major strategic thrusts of this company going to be?

   • How do you evaluate the effectiveness of this organization?

   • What would you suggest that I learn more about in order to understand this organization?

- How would you describe the corporation's performance over the last few years?

- If you were to identify the top three issues facing this organization right now, what would they be?

- What are the key factors in helping this organization reach its near-term objectives?

- What are the major questions this company is dealing with or needs to deal with?

Consider these as starter questions and adapt them to suit your situation. The basic point is to get the executive talking about something she has both knowledge of and interest in—and something also useful to you in finding out where your organization is going.

7. Talk with line executives about their jobs and the organization's directions rather than your job and what you ought to do. They know more about the former and less about the latter. Whenever they do talk about what you do, it is most useful for them to tell you about the outputs they expect from your department. When you ask them what you ought to be doing within your function, you are in effect giving your expertise away. Your questions can be interpreted as meaning that they know or should know how to run your department. That is not the impression you want to convey.

8. Tell those you interview what you are going to do with the results and promise them a summary, or at least a written report. Follow-up leverages your earlier interviews into management support for your mission.

9. Ask the questions in item 6 of your department instead of the company.

One possible result of this process is that you will build the best picture of where the organization you serve is going. One staff manager used her interview data as the basis for showing the top management team that, where they thought they agreed, there was in fact disagreement. That staff manager's synthesis of their thoughts about organizational direction became the starting point for their work on establishing a more unified direction—and allowed the staff manager to be quite influential regarding how her department could help.

Values and Philosophy 7

If the mission defines what we are trying to be, the values and philosophy provide departmental spiritual guidance along the path to that mission. Philosophy and values are in one section because they are a part of each other. Values are those beliefs that you support with your thoughts, words, feelings, and actions. Philosophy might be considered the umbrella that all those values fit under or the sum of the values. As one public relations director said to me, "We have a mission in this department and as we reach out to accomplish it, there are certain values we are going to honor. We believe that the ways in which we reach out to accomplish our mission are as important as the mission itself. That is why we have worked to clarify our values. We revisit these values on a regular basis to make sure that our actions fit with our underlying philosophy and mission." He sees mission as defining his department's unique purpose, and philosophy guiding how they will move toward those purposes. Expressed another way, mission is *what* you are reaching out to be; and philosophy guides *how* you are going to get there. Both are expressed in more ideal terms.

From this point on, we will talk about values, since they make up the philosophy.

This we believe

Exploring values

In the corporate world, we have used the word "value" for years, primarily in relation to the marketplace. We have encouraged consumers to seek "good value." Value has been valued by us. It is another sense of the word that we will explore now. Let's think about personal values as a way of thinking about staff department values. Consider your answers to these questions:

• What do I believe in?

• What is really important to me?

• How are my beliefs different from those of others?

• What do I stand for?

These questions are aimed at the heart of your values. Their answers clarify who you are in terms of what has primary meaning for you in your life. Your answers are yardsticks by which you decide upon daily actions. By definition, these answers are important to you.

Some samples of values that individuals often hold might help clarify this point. If you could only select one item from the following list, which one would be most important to you?

Good health	Long-term relationships	Material wealth
Self-sufficiency	Intellectual growth	Prestige
Athletic ability	Strong marriage	Sex appeal

Notice the considerations you went through in making the choice. You were involved in clarifying what you valued; you briefly considered (from a rather limited field) what is important to you in your life.

Value criteria

Still considering values from your individual perspective, here are seven criteria that the value experts* have compiled as a measure for determining whether you hold a value or not:

*L. E. Raths, M. Harmin, and S. Simon, *Values and Teaching* (Columbus, Ohio: C. E. Merrill Publishing Company, 1966).

Choosing:	1. freely
	2. from alternatives
	3. after thoughtful consideration of the conse-
	quences of each alternative
Prizing:	4. cherishing, being happy with the choice
	5. willing to affirm the choice publicly
Acting:	6. doing something with the choice
	7. repeatedly, in some pattern of life

Apply these seven criteria to your choice from that short list in the earlier paragraph and see how it fits: Is it something you chose freely after having considered alternatives and their consequences? Is it a choice you are happy with and willing to speak up for? Have you followed that choice with action through time that has impacted your life? If so, then this is one of the many values you hold in your life.

For example, at the time I am writing this book, many people in the country are valuing good health. After thoughtful considera- tion of the alternatives, they are choosing to speak up for and habitually act in healthy ways. They are smoking less, exercising more, eating better, drinking lighter, and breathing deeper. The "good health" value is being chosen by enough individuals over a long enough time that businesses are based on it, school curricula are altered, new professions have been founded, and old ones have expanded. We could say that this country is valuing good health. Without exaggeration we can say some organizations are valuing good health. When a company builds a health and fitness center for its employees and adapts it policies and procedures to encourage employees to use the center, that is valuing.

The "good health" examples at an individual, national, and cor- porate level offer a convenient parallel to the staff department ap- plications of values we will explore in the rest of this section. Just as you are strengthened as a person by being clearer about what your values are, so too is a staff department strengthened through clarifying what it stands for. Sorting out what is most important to the life of a staff department is complicated because so many individuals are involved; their personal values need to be integrated with the department's values for the department values to have meaning. If you think this involves a lot of meeting time, discussion, and hard work, you are right. The time and effort it takes can only be justified by the expectation that the outcomes will serve departmental performance better than if nothing were done in pursuit of values. So do not see what follows as prescriptive in the sense that every staff department ought to go through this. Instead, see it as an alternative that has helped others pull themselves together and define the underlying foundations that their mutual direction and effort rest upon.

Let's apply the following questions to the seven value criteria listed earlier. When should these be clarified for a staff department? Who should be involved? How do we do it? Let me briefly explore the answers to each of these questions.

When should values be clarified for a staff department?

1. When the department renders a service that is hard to measure in tangible ways. For example, an employee-assistance department offering counselling services.

2. When department members must represent the department independently and operate without the guidance of a set procedure or rules. For example, a public affairs department with representatives in contact with local politicians and public interest groups.

3. When department members are more idealistic in their approach to large organizational life and hope to reach those ideals through their work. For example, an organizational development department with internal consultants who have strong beliefs about how this corporation should function.

4. When the most significant rewards people expect from their work are internal rather than external. For example, when a social service center has no money for rewards but can emphasize the internal rewards of contribution to the community, helping those in need, and making a small but important difference in people's lives.

5. When a department is in conflict over the ways in which they carry out their functions, but seems to have some unexpressed but important underlying values that everyone

respects. For example, when an advertising department stops fighting among themselves to clarify what they believe in together and then uses that base to explore constructive ways of working together in the future.

6. When a department is changing its directions, services, or professional staff. For example, when a legal department that has been totally decentralized is putting lawyers in field locations.

Ideally, everyone should be involved who has an investment in the values—in other words, everyone who will be expected to act on the values or support them in significant ways. But how do you do this? Practically, you often cannot get fifty-seven people in one room in intelligent conversation for a day, so we need to look for involvement alternatives that include people in relation to their investment in the values.

Who should be involved?

1. As department manager, you can work out the values by yourself and promulgate them. Useful to you; not so useful to others.

2. You can assemble your top team to work out the values and then test the draft on the rest of your invested population.

3. You can ask for ideas in writing from the whole department on what your basic values seem to be, accompanying the request with a short piece describing values and giving a few examples.

4. You can have individuals describe what values they are trying to meet through their work. Have them do this in groups of from four to eight and search out those common values that are then reported to the whole group.

5. You can come up with your own alternative approach to values in your group by talking with them about values, finding out if they want to clarify them, and getting their help on how to do it.

What are commonly held values?

Some commonly held values are listed below. They take on much more meaning when developed by a group.

1. *Performance*. We believe in performing our work in ways that meet the organization's expectations of us and each individual's expectations of himself or herself.

2. *Interdependence*. We are capable individuals who choose to rely on each other's resources to get our work done. We recognize that we can do our work better by using each other than we can do it alone.

3. *Commitment*. We value the individual commitment that comes with participation in deciding what work we will do and how we will do it.

4. *Authority*. Within our department we give authority to those whose knowledge and skill contribute to excellent work; we respect the authority that comes with position.

5. *Responsibility*. We believe that responsibility should be given to the individual or group that is expected to deliver the results.

6. *Accountability*. We perform best when we know what is expected of us and are accountable for the outcomes of our work.

7. *Choice*. We use our talents better when we can decide what we will do in our work.

8. *Risk*. As the primary representatives of our profession in this organization, we expect to give guidance to others that, though helpful in intent, may risk our standing.

9. *Excellence*. Our work is first judged against our internal standards and then judged against the company's expectations.

This list of values relates to those ways of working that might be honored in any staff (or line) organization. Your department's unique staff responsibilities would certainly be reflected in the values you evolve. Reading through your values, I ought to be able to tell whether you are a purchasing department, a graphics group, or an accounting function. Just as your individual values define who you are by stating where you stand, so too it is with departmental values.

The list that you build must be honored with more than words. To be effective and to live, values must be preached, discussed, even ritualized through time. They become standards for daily actions. Management refers to them and models them. Support of the values deserves positive recognition. The department's mission, strategy, plans, and objectives all need to be consistent with the values. The values also need to be reconsidered formally at least once a year, both to check the fit and to make sure we still support them.

A point that applies to visions and mission, values and philosophy is that you never get there. They are established as ideals that are just beyond our reach and that inspire us to higher-level behaviors and aspirations. This is not to say that we never have any success in reaching for these ideals. There will certainly be moments when we have obviously acted in ways that move us toward mission accomplishment while modelling our values, and that moment passes quickly. And we still have the same demanding visions, mission, philosophy, and values to measure this new moment against. I would go so far as to say that if there is anything in your vision, mission, philosophy, or values that can be accomplished and held onto through time, then it probably doesn't belong there. It is not that it is unimportant; it just belongs lower on the hierarchy, in support of the ideals you aspire to.

Values need lengthy discussion because they are important, intangible, and difficult to share. Quantifiable company objectives communicate with us quickly; we understand the dollars, the pro-

You never get there

duct units, or the workdays allotted. The clarity of their meaning reduces the need to talk about them: $5,000,000 is not $3,468,942. We understand the quantifiable in the same way, with little discussion. We grow to understand mission, philosophy, and values together through long, time-consuming discussion. Someone who was not there will read what we have written and likely see it as motherhood/fatherhood statements. But we will know what it really means. We know the bond of understanding and feeling we shared as we left that mission/values meeting. We know the trust that was built. We know how accountable each of us feels to upholding the philosophy we developed.

Because of the nebulous nature of values, we also need to talk about what these might be like in action. What kinds of things would we see ourselves doing differently? How would we know from watching someone whether they were supporting the mission or not? What management behaviors demonstrate the values we have agreed to? All our hard work can result in nothing but slogans if the more philosophical part is not followed with actions.

You know the truth of this as an individual. Every boy scout has to convert concepts like honest, trustworthy, loyal, and brave into some kind of action to get his badges. The work that you do as a manager is given meaning by the mission it supports and the values it respects. Without them, the work becomes meaningless. You will lose your motive for being and doing. There is an interdependence of the actions/behaviors and the mission/values; they need each other for meaning. The next four chapters in this part of the book need these first two on visions, mission, value, and philosophy.

Another element of mission and philosophy is the marketing perspective available to you. My belief is that missions and philosophy should be written initially for internal staff department consumption and later altered for the rest of the organization to understand. If we worry too early about how our mission will "play" with top management, we may end up with a statement that better represents what we think *they* think we should be rather than what *we* think we should be. Write it on your own terms and then change it so that it plays well with management or whomever. Changing it here reflects our need to help others understand us in their terms, without altering what we are about.

Goals and Strategy 8

If mission defines the organization's unique purpose and direction, then goals and strategy provide structured guidance toward accomplishing that mission. From the many ways you could attempt to fulfill your mission, you must choose *the* way. The strategic plan documents the way you have chosen to reach a limited number of goals over the next three to five years.

Reach out

For most of us, today's performance expectations are clear: do more, with less, and fast! Meeting these expectations can be a job and a half—and we still may not be doing an effective job. To be effective you need to expand your perspective, not narrow it. You need to reach out on either side to understand more of the organization you work in and its environment. You need horizontal breadth of understanding as much as vertical depth in your function to be an effective staff manager. The risk is that you will listen too much to what is expected and too much to what has made you successful in the past.

Strategy considerations

As natural as it may seem to pay attention to what you want and your company wants, it is far from all you need to experience success. Do listen to the expectations of your management. Do listen to your professional staff experience. And do not prioritize what you are going to actually do until you have considered these questions:

1. What is this business all about and what are management's expectations for it over the next three to five years?

2. How could your department have an impact on the direction of the business—both in terms of helping establish its direction and also reaching out to accomplish what is intended?

3. How does your department relate to other staff functions in purpose, strategy, and methodology as well as customers served?

4. How do you personally want to affect the direction of the business? What professional contribution do you want to make? How important is it to you?

5. How well are you serving the organization right now? By its standards? By your own standards? How would you improve?

6. How are the answers to the last question altered when you

consider what you believe your function really ought to be doing for the corporation?

7. What have you done and what could you do to help the organization better understand how your function might be used?

8. What projects do you have underway that aid in moving the company to using your department better than it is now using it?

9. How are you developing your staff into a perspective on your staff function that reflects the broader orientation reflected in the above questions?

10. What other questions does this short list bring to mind in your corporate situation?

These questions are different from most of those we were considering when discussing mission and philosophy and values. These ten questions move us to begin to convert our ideals to orchestrated action; they suggest establishing a handful of primary goals and strategizing to reach them.

They ask us to step back and reach out to broaden our understanding of the marketplace, the company, other staff departments, and our own department. And we do all of this while still considering the demands made on us by our management and by our own desires. It is a tall order to measure up to. I think we need to try to balance all these perspectives, accepting that our attempt may be a bit idealistic. If we don't try, we are lost. We may become very good technicians, or good project leaders, or great supervisors, but our function's direction will be completely in the hands of the line managers we are reacting to. And all we will ever do is react.

Remember that old line, "When you are up to your ass in alligators, it's damned difficult to drain the swamp." True—and that is just what we must do. Staff management is not a choice between swamp draining or alligator harvesting. Somehow the staff manager must do both at the same time to be successful. This means keeping both perspectives in mind simultaneously. Somehow we must react and respond to the problems of today. And while doing that we must decide what we want and anticipate what the organization will need for tomorrow . . . so that today's actions consider both the present and future perspectives.

And that is what strategy is about: simultaneous swamp draining and alligator harvesting. The emphasis is on the former without neglecting the reality of the latter.

Determining your products and markets

Consider your function from a marketing perspective.* What would a marketing person say about the products and services you offer in your corporate marketplace? What new directions would market-oriented questions point your department toward? Consider these marketing thoughts:

1. What is your product? What are your services? Who are your customers? Who would you like as customers? What other products or services would you like to offer? Are these questions unusual for you? If they are, there may be some real potential benefits to you in answering them. Looking at yourself as an independent service bureau with a sole customer to satisfy is significantly different for many of us than seeing ourselves as managers of one of many staff departments in a large corporation.

2. Are you product-driven? Service-driven? Market-driven? The first two have a heavy focus on providing this product or that service especially well. Their focus is on doing what we do better and better. The market-driven perspective is focussed on what the market needs, will need, could need, and won't need. The organization adapts to that market need.

*John Simonds helped with these thoughts.

3. Have you asked what your market needs lately? When did you last interview your customers about the products and services they are currently getting and what they might want in the future?

4. What's the competition doing? What are your customers' alternatives to what they are currently getting from you? Competition to an inside staff function sounds ridiculous to many of us, but not to the information processing department since the arrival of the personal computer and its associated software.

5. If you were going to sell your product based on customer needs, how would you promote it? To whom? And when? Think about some of those products you know the organization needs but is not requesting from you. How do you create awareness of that need in the organization?

6. When was the last time you test-marketed a service? Have you ever tried something out on some small part of the organization, surveyed the results, and used that data to tailor your service to the needs of the customer?

7. What can you do to gain credibility in the marketplace? What services gain easy access to the customer and open the door for other services that are less immediately palatable?

There are at least four ways to develop business for your staff in the organization. First, you can wait for the business to come to you. Second, you can establish policies and procedures that require business to come your way. Third, you can go out into the organization and sell your product and services. And fourth, you can research the organization's needs and market yourself to those needs. Each of these approaches requires different supporting actions and has different consequences, according to the organization you are serving. Each has implications for your departmental strategy.

A strategic planning process

Let's explore a strategic planning process that has been useful to me as a staff manager and as a consultant to staff managers.

1. *Start with your departmental vision and mission, philosophy and values.* This is where strategic planning begins. This assumes that in addition to having thought about what you really want this staff function to be, you have explored how this relates to the larger organization. And you are in concert with that large organization you serve. As earlier chapters have expressed, a mission and philosophy are helpful in bringing a focus to your efforts, but they are not enough. There are many ways of going about accomplishing that mission, and you lack agreement on how to do that. This is where the strategic planning process comes in.

2. *What do you look like five years out?* Based on your mission and assuming good fortune, where would you like to be five years from now? You know what you want your department to be to the organization; your mission has expressed that well. Now, if the gods were with you, what would your department be doing five years from now that indicates you have moved toward mission accomplishment? Get really specific here:

   • What services would you be offering?

   • Who would your clients be?

   • How would you be structured?

   • Where would you report?

   • What would be your priorities?

   • What contribution would you be making to the organization?

   • How would others be using your resources?

Paint a verbal picture of how you would like the department to be operating five years from now. When you get this picture refined and agreed upon by the top people in your department, you have a target to work toward. In effect you have said, "We decided on a mission that was in keeping with our values. That is important to us, and we know that we have to move toward action if we want some parts of our professional dreams to become reality. So the first step we have taken is to envision how things will be five years from now for this department, assuming our mission is our guide and luck is with us. We will use this five-years-out picture to guide our planning."

The last line is an important one: use the future as a guide for planning. Describing the future you want and honoring it with related plans are essential to strategic planning. The future is not to be dealt with as simply a projection of today into tomorrow. The future is not simply past performance analyzed and patterned and extended into next year, at least not the future I am talking about. The future is full of possibilities, hopes, dreams, wants, desires, and alternatives, and many of these are quite different from those of yesterday and today. What you want for your department may bear no resemblance to what you now have—and that is legitimate within this strategic planning process. We are looking for ways to bring your dreams into reality, not to continue with "business as usual."

3. *Identify goals.* With the verbal picture you painted of your department five years out, and your knowledge of what exists today, you are in a good position to identify key result areas that *must* be acted upon to realize your five-year picture. There will be only a few areas where it is critically important that goals be established and action be taken. Label these key areas and tie down your goals in each as tightly as you can. These few goals are the base for strategic planning.

4. *Build plans.* What do you need to do over the next five years to reach your goals? Step back from the whole five years and lay out a plan for what you will need to do each year to be where you want to be five years from now. For those

of you accustomed to thinking in terms of next year, or next month, or today, this will feel awkward. It requires letting go (temporarily) of today's pressures, stepping back from your work, and laying out a plan toward what you want to have happen. It will look something like this:

This planning is strategic in that it recognizes the needs of tomorrow, it is aimed at accomplishment of a future that you envision, and it is used in the guidance of today's actions.

The risks at this point in the process are many. It is easy to lose sight of the future we want by planning our lower priorities. Instead, know that you increase your chances of influencing the future when you focus on those few top priorities. Another risk is allowing reality to move in on you too quickly and therefore aspiring to less. Another risk is getting into too much detail in describing specific actions that you will take two, three, or four years from now. At this point it is enough to state the general action. For example, decentralize the department, or input to the corporate strategic planning process, or diagnose a need of the marketing division.

This planning process needs to be done with the acceptance of the fact that much of what you decide will be changed as the *real* future unfolds. As difficult as it may sound, you need to invest your planning energy in laying out what you want to do over the next five years to move your department to its desired state. Know that these plans will allow you to be more alert to what is happening around you and, in turn, adapt the plans to deal with what is really happening. Strategic planning increases awareness of the present so the present can be dealt with in terms of the desired future (rather than just in terms of the recent past).

5. *What do you need to do during this next year?* In the last step I cautioned you about too much detail; now is the time to let your need for specificity loose. Plan what you are going to do in this next year to reach your desired state five years from now and do it in as much detail as you plan anything else that is important in your department. Lay out specific

objectives and action plans; assign responsibility; set up review processes; this is important! Take into account the other forces acting in the organization that may not support what you want to do. Deal with these forces through communication, education, confrontation, negotiation, collaboration, or whatever you need to use to move your strategy ahead in operational terms. This is the step where dealing with realities is particularly important because you are about to do something in the real present. This step probably links up well with the annual operational planning that your department does, at least that is the intent. At some point, the longer-range strategic thinking you have been doing must be integrated with what is already going on in the organization. We will talk more about this in a later chapter on objectives and plans.

The steps discussed above link vision, mission, philosophy, and values with strategy and goals. The methods for completing these steps are affected by the people you involve, how you involve them, your staff department's stature within the organization, the pressures on you, and your need to strategize. A few more comments for staff managers who are beginning to think more strategically:

Perspectives on strategy

1. *The process is as important as the product.* After all your work is finished, you have a plan laid out before you. This plan is valuable. Also valuable is the additional clarity you have about your directions and what you will do to get there. Your motivation is up as you see ways to get what you want. Your staff professionals are more focussed and committed to the extent that they have helped develop this plan. Because of all the thinking you have done, you are more acutely aware of what is going on around you in the organization; you will see actions that impact your plans which previously would have gone unnoticed.

2. *You must develop strategy whether the company does it or not.* Far from complaining about the company's lack of strategic direction, your thrust is to identify your own direction. If the company does not have one that is expressed, then

develop your own and test it on the management. Your strategic thinking may help them clarify what they want. So don't complain; take advantage of the opportunity.

3. *Link your strategy to the company's.* This is implicit in the earlier work we did on mission, and needs to be emphasized here: there should be an obvious relationship between what your staff department is doing over the next five years and where the company is going—and it needs to be a positive relationship. As a more formal part of this, get your work on strategy linked up with the company's strategic planning process. Find a way to get yourself included in the annual strategy rounds, whatever their present value might be. Then use your inclusion in this process to educate senior management on your priorities. You may even have a staff responsibility (e.g., human resources or accounting) that deserves to be included as one of the considerations all planning managers work through as they do their strategic planning.

4. *Pay attention.* Set up listening posts that give you information related to your strategic plans. You need an early warning system that informs you more quickly so you have time to think before you act.

5. *Build support for your strategies.* Understanding of your plans is support; it is a form of power unavailable to those whose strategies are undeveloped or unheard of in management circles. So initially seek understanding and follow this with agreement, then action. Do not expect action from people who do not understand or agree. As foolish as this may sound in writing, in *fact* we often ask others to act in support of our actions before they understand or agree.

6. *Strategic planning is different for a staff function—but not that different.* In methodology, it is about the same as what a senior line manager might go through. In content it is obviously dependent on the larger organization. But in that regard it does not differ from what the corporation faces. It is dependent on the larger environment, the marketplace,

the economy, the customer. If anything, the staff strategic planner should have an easier job because the corporation's world is a little easier to get a conceptual hold on than the whole world. The staff strategizer's job differs in that it is often not seen as important to do by the important people in the organization. You have to bring your own importance to it because your boss and the corporate systems often do not require you to work through the process. The advantage in this position is that you can strategize in your own way, unconstrained by the narrow financial emphasis of the corporate process—if yours is anything like most I know.

7. *If there is anything important to you that you do not now have and you want in the long term, plan for it!* For a staff department, a corporation, or an individual, this is true. It is not enough to think about it, gripe about it, wish, or pray— though all of these can be important. Bring your intentions to reality by planning and action.

I magine a staff department that is highly skilled and always at the ready position, poised for action, and waiting for the word from their line customers. It's as if they were saying, "We are here. We are capable. We are paying attention. You just tell us where to go and what to do, and we will do it well." It is not unlike your local fire station. When the alarm sounds, everyone flies into action and does their job well. But they wait for the alarm to sound; they do not sound it. And they do not go out and set fires; they wait. Someone else takes the initiative for them to go to work.

There are staff departments who function this way and many who ought to function this way. Some of our responsibilities are so entwined with other people's actions that we must wait. It is not as if we do not do anything while we are waiting. We get ready,

Proactive or reactive?

make sure our equipment works, polish our skills, or help our customers learn what we do and when to call us. Support functions like graphics, word processing, the cafeteria, and aviation are examples that seem to fit with the more reactive stance. They are very much in service to others and perform important responsibilities by being ready, quick, flexible, and patient with their customers.

Proactivity is at the other end of the initiative spectrum. It involves anticipating the future, taking the initiative, and going to the customer with information or services before the customer comes to you. It can mean speaking out when you have not been asked to or being an advocate for a corporate position on a key issue. Departments like public affairs, personnel, auditing, and accounting often find themselves faced with proactive alternatives.

We are all capable of a range of departmental behavior. There are opportunities to be proactive, reactive, or variations in between. The more important point has to do with our awareness. Are we consciously choosing to be a reactive function and making the most of that particular strategy? Or do we see ourselves as strategically proactive, as taking the action to our customers, not waiting for them to come to us? Are we aware of and building on the strength that comes from being aware of the strategy we are using? Not being aware of our strategy, and not consciously choosing, means missed opportunities.

Top down or bottom up?

This strategic consideration is likely not foreign to you. Perhaps you reflected it when you said, "If only top management were behind us, we would have no trouble at all in getting this implemented." Or "Let's try it out in one plant and build on our success there." Both of these statements relate to strategic decisions we are accustomed to making on individual projects.

Similar considerations are involved in developing the strategic thrust of the department. As a staff department manager who is interested in moving toward a mission, you must decide where you are going to build your power base. The polarized choice is between aligning yourself with the power of the top management or building your power with the customer groups farther down in the hierarchy. In practice you will find yourself working at both levels and in between, but for our purposes, let's consider the extremes.

The top-down strategy requires reporting higher, having access higher, and being accountable higher. Consequences of the top-down strategy can include:

Top down

- You will be very visible to the people who make important decisions about the organization and also about your future. You must be prepared to be in the spotlight.

- Successes are big successes and mistakes are big mistakes.

- Your goals and directions must be very clear to you, and you must be consistent in your articulation and pursuit of them.

- This is not a strategy to select if you are less knowledgeable or less experienced in your functional responsibilities.

- You need both an understanding and an appreciation of organizational politics. If you lack these qualities, there is probably much going on at the top that you will not understand or have access to.

- You cannot select this strategy just because it makes sense; it also has to fit with your individual style.

- The way you do things is very important at the top. Accept this as fact. It is not that the way you do things is not important at the bottom; it just has lower risk and potentially different consequences.

- The upper spheres of management are inhabited by people with a high power orientation—that is what it takes to get things done. You need to appreciate these people, to respect them, to be successful with them.

- If you want the quick big impact, you must be willing to take the big risks that come with working top down.

Bottom up

The bottom-up strategy assumes reporting lower and focussing lower in the organization. Its consequences can include:

- You can learn as you go. If you are less skilled as a manager or in your functional arena, you have time to build your skills.

- You can build from small successes and take on larger projects when you are ready for them.

- Failures do not make as much organizational difference.

- Your customers will appreciate you. Many of them are used to not getting any staff appreciation, so having you acknowledge their importance feels good to them, and they may pass this on to you.

- It is easier to alter your department's direction when you have not made the big commitment at the top. You can feel your way until it becomes more visible.

- If you like to work and see short-term results, there is a lot of reward available to you in this bottom-up strategy. It is hands-on; you will be familiar with the details of many projects and much of the company. It is a good way to learn more about the company while you are learning more about managing and/or your function.

- If you are looking for big, fast change in the organization, forget it. This approach requires a lot of patience and perseverance.

- Down here, you lose a sense of large organizational priorities as you get preoccupied with the trees and leaves rather than the forest.

- The people you work with—your customers—have a high

achievement orientation. They see politics as a dirty word and cannot appreciate its possibly positive uses in the organization.

• Along with having less power, you also have less status in most organizations. Focussing on the projects, systems, and tasks needed to make the working end of the organization work does not get the topside recognition it deserves.

Objectives and Plans

9

Annual plans, management by objectives, operational plans, budgeting—these are the things that objectives and plans are made of. Most of us know about this level of planning since it is focussed on the near term—usually the next year—and since our organizations require something of us that we honor with some thought and lots of paper. Many of us have well-developed operational planning skills; we know how to do it, and it does help us keep track of where our department is going. The weakness of many staff operational plans is the lack of a larger strategy. The result can be a fine job of planning in a short-term and narrow reactive framework.

Too much planning starts from today or yesterday without balancing these time periods against the future. The fact that you and I plan does not mean we are not reactive. We are capable of planning a reaction to a line management request; we can do it both quickly and in some detail, taking pride in what good planners we are and fooling ourselves all along. Purposeful reactions are reactions nevertheless.

What will we do?

Responsibility for a staff function requires that we look at what is being asked of us and see how it fits with our mission and strategy (not to mention philosophy and values). We should question instructions devoting our resources to projects that are not part of our plans. Management expects and deserves to hear our guidance. When we withhold that guidance we in effect tell management that they know better, know more about what we should be doing than we do. Respecting their position does not include withholding our expertise.

We need not plan everything we do. A significant part of the staff management job is to be responsive to today. This varies from function to function. It would be easier if we knew that all of our work or none of our work needed to be planned. The truth is that some of it does and some of it doesn't. The truth is that sometimes we must react and at other times we must reflect and plan before acting. So we are stuck with paying attention all of the time, doing both the strategic thinking and the day-to-day reacting at the same time. (Yes, swamp draining and alligator harvesting again.)

Objectives and plans are focussed on what you must do now to achieve your goals and support your strategies. It is tied up with the who, what, where, when, and how of the next year. It is measurable in its actions and outcomes. Without these objectives and plans, your visions of the future are never acted on in the way that they deserve. It requires discipline to pay attention to it while all the world around you is apparently bent on distracting you from what you think is most important. Objectives and plans are expected to change as they meet the reality of today. Since they are plans toward something, when reality intrudes with its own truth, we need to design new ways of reaching for what we want while considering what today is asking of us. This means modifying those old objectives and plans that were based on predictions of the future that didn't quite come true. So earlier planning has served us well if it allows us to see and adapt to the present while we still reach out for the future we want.

Goals are to strategies, in the long term, as objectives are to plans in the short term. Goals and objectives are what we will do; strategies and plans are how we will do them. The more immediate objectives and plans are quite measurable; goals and strategies are usually less measurable.

Today's work is so compelling that we do not take time to think about tomorrow. Most of us take some pride in just being able to handle what is in front of us, in being responsive to our clients across the organization. Just staying on top of things is enough! But it isn't. At least it isn't enough if we have some staff aspirations that take us beyond "business as usual."

While we are plowing through today's work, we need to be looking down the road at what is coming in our direction. What will be asked of us tomorrow? What does today's work have to do with next month's reports? What new organizational systems, structures, policies, and procedures will be affecting us in the near term? How can we get ready? How can we help our management get ready? What do we want them to be thinking about now so they will be ready for later?

One of the best places to move beyond being reactive and responsive to today is in relation to the organization's planning cycle. Nowadays almost everybody has one. Whether they use it or not, value it or not, is something else again. For those of you in organizations that plan ahead at least a year at a time: When does the management begin this process? And what are they planning for? For example, the five-year planning cycle starts in June and feeds into the operational planning and budgeting for next year, which starts in early September. Make sense? Note the same cycle within your organization.

Next question: What department, which position, which person do you want to influence in this planning cycle? How would you like some part of their plans to read if you could have it your way? For example: "I want Sales' long-range plan to reflect the increasing effect of the computer on the numbers and skills of salespeople in that department." Now, knowing what the department's planning cycle is and knowing how you would like to influence the outcome, you are in a good position to initiate action that helps the Sales VP plan for the future.

Get ahead of their cycle and inform their cycle. Work in relation to the planning process they respect. Use their own process to introduce new ideas to them at the time they can take the more constructive action.

Anticipation and initiation

Get ahead of them

Take one example. The technical training department of a chemicals company saw that the future could possibly make great demands on its resources. They knew the company was growing, the technology was changing, and the prerequisite skills took years to develop. Repeated questions of management about "what do you want us to do?" produced no unified response. The technical training manager anticipated the impending work about to descend on her department and decided to initiate action to get the line organization to deal with this upcoming situation. Using the corporation's planning process timing as a starting point, the manager went to the top three levels of the company to gather information about the future of the company—as they saw it—plus the implications of this future for the skills of the people in the company.

Not only did the training manager gather a lot of interesting and useful information, she also put together a verbal picture of what this organization will look like from a people perspective five years hence. She presented that as input to the company's planning process at precisely the right point—while executives were thinking about their plans but hadn't made them yet. The result? Plans were quite obviously impacted when contrasted with the previous year, which affected the priorities of the technical training department. An important side benefit: the verbal picture the training manager had put together was the first composite picture assembled and agreed to by the executive level. It resulted in much discussion and agreement that a similar approach should be followed by the executive group *before* putting together their strategic plan.

Activity vs. results

Look at your department's objectives for the coming period. Is there an obvious relationship between these departmental objectives and the core mission, strategy, and objectives of the organization? Are they written and pursued in such a way that the relationship between your staff actions and the organizational result is as clear as possible—to a line executive? If the president of your company stopped by your office this afternoon and asked you to tell her what your group does to help this organization get better results, what would you answer? How satisfied would you be with the response? And how about the president?

Too often staff people think in terms of the functions they perform as ends in themselves rather than as means to larger organizational ends. Processing 523 contracts this quarter may have meaning as a goal in the contracts section, but what does it have to do with where we are going as an organization? I am not questioning whether it has anything to do with its overall direction—in fact, I assume it does, but how would that be evident to a line executive looking in? And would that line perspective be seen and felt as relevant by the people in the contracts section? I hope so!

Notice the language that is respected by the line. Notice the orientation toward action and results, and copy it. Talk their language; think closer to their ways of thought; appreciate more of their perspective. Tie your key objectives to their key objectives. Visibly show the interlocking nature of what you are doing with and for them. Negotiate your objectives with managers working on priority company objectives so that they are depending on you to help them get their job done. They need you. If you don't do your part, they are in trouble. Make sure you are working on important projects. Start collecting your possible objectives in your line customers' offices, not in your own. You can always ask yourself, "What do we want to do this year?" Ask that later, after you find out what your clients need this year. Consider it all—your needs, their wants, the organization's direction—and then decide.

Set up staff objectives that look like line objectives

Systems and Methods

10

All the processes we have discussed (vision, mission, values, philosophy, goals, strategy, objectives, plans) do not happen without a framework. We have to assure ourselves that we will return to consider our priorities on a regular basis, and this is where a planning system comes in. Systems help assure that the big priorities are not crowded out by the little ones, that the important is not overshadowed by the urgent. Managing systematically assures us that we have the proper inputs we need in time to make more critical management decisions related to mission and strategy.

For example, we need to reconsider our mission, philosophy, and strategies at least once a year. And that must be built into our planning system if we are to do it when it is time to do it. It is not easy to gather information and your key people together for one to three days to reconsider departmental direction—and without building that meeting into a systematic framework it is unlikely to happen. Link that review to the corporation's planning process so that you are ahead of what the organization is doing rather than behind and waiting to be told what you must do. Get ahead of the process to give you the chance to influence others before their planning is

**Planning
systems**

complete—rather than arriving late and attempting to alter what they have carved in stone.

I think the department's objectives and plans need to be reviewed at least quarterly. As department manager you should at least read through the plans for this year and see how the department has done during the last three months. What have we accomplished? What have we not taken into account? What needs modifying? Whose individual objectives are affected and how? What needs recognition? Reinforcing? Correcting? And how do I need to deal with the answers to these questions in order to build people's understanding, commitment, and support? What do I want to tell my boss about all this and how could I involve my boss?

This quarterly review keeps operational plans alive, which in turn increases everyone's investment in the planning process. If your department's plans die in a drawer, so will the individual plans of the people who work for you. And others will know that the plans you assemble are an administrative artifact. Granted, many people in the organization just go through the motions because they see the planning required of them as an intrusive and useless process. Considering the way they approach it, they are right. But you can make the planning process live by giving it systematic attention and by linking it to the motivation and performance of the people in your department. The mission and values tie the process described here to motivation; the elements of strategy and planning tie it to performance. It is a process that recognizes the whole person and attempts to draw on the aspirations, ideals, abilities, and energies of that person. Systems that do less will be seen as unrealistic by the people carrying them out.

Systems are the action frameworks that tie the major managerial elements together. Systematic thinking and action move our management concepts from cloudy visions to down-to-earth implementation. And, from a staff manager's perspective, they give us the initiative with our customers so we are thinking out in front of them rather than planning to catch up.

Systems "shoulds"

One of your primary duties as manager is to monitor, update, and maintain the planning system your department uses to allow it to be a focussed, collaborative unit moving in a single direction.

Here are some biases that have helped me build, maintain, and improve upon the planning systems I have used as a manager:

- The systems should allow you to do your job better than you could without them.

- The systems should provide you with data critical to the management of your department—and on a timely basis so you can act on it.

- The systems should help those working for you influence the direction of the department and know that they have that opportunity.

- These systems should assure your people that they will know how their performance fits with what is expected of them in their work. They will know their work is relevant to both departmental and corporate directions.

- The same systems should assure that individuals with expertise will be brought together to work on the problems that need that expertise.

- The systems should let people know what is going on in time for them to use the information in their work.

- The systems should require department members to take on a responsible role as a part of the departmental team.

- The systems should treat individuals as adults expected to speak up on behalf of the department, themselves, and others to aid in departmental and individual performance.

That is a lot of "shoulds," and they do reflect my perspective on what you want these planning systems to do. You no doubt have some "shoulds" of your own. What you "should" do is to figure out what they are and write them down.

Methods for management

Methods, elements, mechanisms, tools—these are all words I have considered as labels for this section about management hierarchy. I am searching for the best word to describe that collection of planned interactions within a planning system that allow a staff manager to build mission statements, to put together this year's plan, to assess individual performance, and to help people look ahead in their careers. What are the various methods you can use? What are those discrete, planned activities that the department uses to assure itself that it is performing toward organizational results?

Here is a list that I think you ought to be conversant with:

- Company review
- Departmental planning
- Problem-solving and decision-making meetings
- Information meetings
- Staff council
- Individual performance planning meetings
- Individual progress reviews
- Individual appraisal sessions
- Individual salary discussions
- Individual development discussions

With these tools at your disposal, plus skills in using these tools, you will be ready for most of the more important management meetings you face during a typical year.

Company review

A primary element of any staff planning system is interfacing with the corporate management team. They represent all of the people whom you serve and who have the right to know what you are doing, how it is going, and what you plan to do. Think in terms of meeting at least twice a year to present your directions and accomplishments to them. An important benefit is the endorsement they provide. This helps you in sorting out your priorities for the coming performance period. Your review of your work naturally focusses on results that they have declared important for the company. If you do not do this now, consider going after it, knowing that it involves visibility, risk, and power.

These semiannual meetings are held off-site, are one to three days long, and give the top six to twelve people the chance to step back from what is going on and look at how well they are doing it. Think in terms of two meetings a year built around the company's planning cycle. The first meeting should precede the planning process in the company by enough time to allow your staff function to both collect data and influence line departments before their own recommendations are made.

Typical agenda items for this meeting include:

- The state of the company

- The state of the department

- Review of the departmental mission and strategic plan

- Roles and responsibilities

- The structure of the department in relation to corporate needs

- Management systems of this department

- Pressing opportunities and problems for the coming year

- Departmental management

- Team effectiveness

This meeting often involves a consultant from outside your department who keeps the group on the course they decided upon and helps them look at how they work together.

About six months later comes a meeting in which the same group takes a look at what you have actually accomplished and still wish to accomplish as a department during the year. This is the time to update those departmental operational plans. This can usually be accomplished in one day, but other items for the agenda (like those listed in the previous paragraph) have a way of asserting their priority. Plan on two days for this review, retrench, and regroup meeting.

Problem-solving and decision-making meetings

These meetings are preceded by an action-oriented agenda which states each agenda item, the responsible person, persons who need to be in attendance for this one item, advanced work that needs to be done by participants, length of time required, the action to be taken, the result expected, and that time in the meeting when all of this will be done. Think of all that in relation to your usual agendas. For many of us, it is quite a departure from the notes on the back of an envelope that we have called an agenda. Sure, it is more work in advance, but remember the frustrations you experience without that preparation and you may find the motivation to do this.

These problem-solving and decision-making meetings are held as required to work on problems, opportunities, and decisions. People attend for that portion of the agenda that is particularly important to them. The composition of the group is changing constantly, according to the authority, expertise, and commitment needed on each agenda item. The department manager must see to it that the agenda gets sent out in advance so people know when to attend and what work to do in preparation for the meeting. The manager must also see that the time constraints are honored and that individuals responsible for action know the specific actions they must take. Minutes of these meetings can be very useful.

Just because it falls to you to make sure all of this happens doesn't mean that as manager you have to do it all. You can delegate it to others, freeing you to be manager as someone else runs the meeting. Hold these meetings as often as needed, knowing that if you go for too long without one they become less important as a management tool. You and your people will also get out of practice. Consider averaging at least one problem-solving and decision-making meeting a month to start with.

Information meetings

Often held weekly and without an agenda, these meetings update your people on what is happening. They are brief (20-30 minutes) and with limited discussion. You and the people reporting directly to cover what has gone on since the last meeting and what will happen before the next one. Often participants leave this meeting for a similar one with their own staff where they both update their staff and get updated on what staff members have been doing and will be doing. The intent is to eliminate unnecessary surprises and to encourage the cooperation of your staff members that can flow out of advanced knowledge of what will be happening. These meetings are most abused by being too long, turning into problem-solving meetings, and losing regular attendees. The department manager must see to it that time is respected, that lengthy discussion is not allowed (people can pursue that outside the meeting if they choose), and that reports are delivered at a brisk pace so the meeting can be adjourned. Making this an early morning stand-up meeting can help.

For staff departments that are decentralized, a staff council can be a useful element of your management system. This council is composed of people reporting directly to you plus people outside your immediate department who carry out the policies and procedures you formulate. The council meets two to four times a year to develop directions for the staff function and learn about your function's directions. Your goal is to include this group in decisions about departmental directions in a way that both assures them influence and educates them on what the department's intentions are.

There are many possible uses of this staff council: a planning body, a problem-solving task force, a decider, a controller, a learning group, a role-defining body, a career development committee. Whatever it is, when it works, you end up with people in the field giving you guidance on where the department might go. Through their involvement, they will be more committed to your direction, and therefore more likely to act in concert with what you want.

Staff council

These one-on-one meetings between you and each person reporting directly to you (and likely between them and theirs) flow out of the annual group meeting discussed in the last section. A once-a-year event, these meetings involve a negotiation between you and the subordinate that balances corporate, departmental, and individual needs and results in a performance plan for the coming year that fits with department objectives and has the individual's commitment behind it. Most of the work is done by the subordinate, based on early discussions between the two of you. An objectives and action plan format agreed to by the department ahead of time assures a focus on tangible outcomes. This meeting is probably at

Individual performance planning meetings

least an hour long; schedule two hours, and if you run out of time make another appointment to finish.

Individual progress reviews

Parallel to the structure that is established for the whole department are the reviews of individual progress. Basically you are checking performance against plan, expecting to make adjustments. The subordinate carries the primary responsibility for preparing for this meeting; he is updating you. This is not an appraisal session and does not go into company records. The meeting is intended to aid performance and give the individual both coaching and recognition for his work.

All of the traditional things you have read about progress reviews could be inserted here. Do all of what the good books say about progress reviews, just do it more often. I think you need to average three progress reviews a year with your staff. This comes to about one full, planned-for, let's-step-back-from-the-work day with each of your people a year. That is not too much time, considering it is the primary one-to-one planning and review you will do. It can pay huge bonuses in the time it saves, the confidence it builds, the confusion it eliminates.

Tell your staff that they can have a progress review whenever they want one. All they have to do is let you know so you can put it on your calendar. They are much closer to their work than you are, and they know when they want to discuss that work with you. Give them responsibility for initiation—without taking away your own power to call a discussion whenever *you* wish. They prepare (80 percent) and you prepare (20 percent) for the discussion; then you meet, with them leading the discussion.

Individual appraisal discussions

These happen about once a year and are probably the type of discussion that most of us are most familiar with. They are required by company policy, and the results are a matter of record. They presently get far too much attention, mostly negative, because they are asked to carry out more functions than they can possibly handle. Done well—that is, following the other individual discussions listed above—they are a piece of cake. They hold no surprises and simply confirm what the two of you already knew from earlier discussions.

Again, give the individual working for you primary responsibility for this discussion. Above all, don't get trapped into an appraisal discussion in which you have to pass on a rating to the person who has already been signed off on by two or three people above you. Instead, talk with the individual before all that official stuff happens, get her thoughts on how she sees her performance, use that information as you make up your mind and submit your thoughts upward, and then, later on, pass the rating back in a rather short discussion. Make sense? It has worked for me. It isn't perfect, but in this difficult appraisal and judgment world nothing is.

Yes, they are an important element of your system. And they take on a different perspective in the context of all the other individual discussions. Now they can be brief and more recognition-oriented. The hard recognition of dollars should obviously tie to the softer recognition you have given through the year in the progress reviews. Standing alone as the *only* recognition an individual gets, the salary discussion takes on a distorted importance that it cannot live up to. So put it in context and it will work much better.

Individual salary discussions

All of the earlier discussions focussed on the past performance or the planned performance. Somewhere in your process you need to consider the individual's future development. Of course, she knows more about what she wants than you do. You can help her think about what the future could hold so she can decide what she wants it to hold. Then the two of you can assess her present abilities against that potential future, and this will give you a good idea about what her developmental priorities are. And you can build that development into her objectives in a way that both she and the organization benefit.

Individual development discussions

I offer these ten methods for managing your staff department as an array to choose from—there are too many to undertake at once. It is simply a listing you can add to, delete from, or alter. If you are going to manage, you are going to use some of the methods on the list. Be as clear with your staff about how you expect to manage them—as clear as you expect them to be with you regarding their professional work.

As I said earlier, involve those who will be most affected by your systems and methods in developing them. Read this section with them, selecting methods and developing a systematic way of managing for yourselves. Next, look at the skills required to manage and participate in a system like the one you have built. Each of the methods mentioned above has some important skills necessary to its proper use. Most of them are one-to-one individual skills or one-to-many group skills. An effective staff manager needs these important people skills.

Structure

How do we divide up the work?

Somewhere between visions and methods, structural considerations are likely to appear. Ideally, structure follows "strategy." In reality, structure is more ongoing. We will now take a look at it as the final important element in managing for results.

When staff organizations are quite small, structure is not a problem. The people doing the work are located close to the people they serve and usually report to those people. For example, the drafting department that reports to the engineering division works exclusively for the engineering division. Everybody involved understands how this works; there are no questions about work priorities that cannot be resolved internally; and the engineering division knows it is in control of drafting. But what happens when drafting is pulled out from engineering and made part of a new, centralized graphics department that reports to the vice-president of administration? The people in engineering are faced with making major adjustments. Their work is now considered against the work of others regarding priorities. They are no longer the sole customer. They may have access to finer equipment. The new structure does make a great difference.

Your experience allows you to tell stories about what has happened to your staff organization as it has grown. Growth in staff functions has introduced organizational considerations that were unheard of when we were small appendages grafted onto the side of a line function. Staff growth has introduced structure as an issue, with these underlying concerns of purpose, effectiveness, and power.

1. *What really is the purpose of your staff function?* Going back to our earlier work on mission and strategy should yield some pretty good answers to this question. Architects say "form follows function." Similarly, in organizations, "structure follows strategy." To carry out the strategy you are pursuing, you need people with appropriate authority and responsibility reporting to you. Suppose, for example, you are responsible for implementing the company's affirmative action program, and you must do this through personnel assistants who report to plant managers spread out across the country. The structure itself says the job is impossible — unless you happen to be the general manager whom the plant managers report to.

2. *How can we structure this function to make it most effective?* This second question obviously relates to the first but is distinct because clarity of purpose does not automatically define what structure is appropriate. There is a range of alternatives, from a highly centralized headquarters structure with high authority to an extremely decentralized staff function reporting to line managers across the corporation with no counterpart at headquarters. There are no right answers to the question of how to effectively structure a staff group. In fact, the answers vary from one staff function to another, and you can learn more from your associates in your profession about the prevailing options than you will learn here. Later on we will deal with the more important considerations in making your choice.

3. *How is power distributed in the structure we choose?* This question gets closer to the crux of the matter: you want to know which structure will give you the power you need to carry out your mission. And the managers who work around you

want to know how your power is compared to their own, because they have some things they want to do, too. This question also legitimizes the expression of power. There is a personal investment that is brought to the surface in discussions of power that may not come up in the questions related to purpose and effectiveness.

The range of organizational possibilities is a continuum, not a bipolar choice. We often talk in terms of centralizing or decentralizing as if it must be one or the other, but there are many options in between. Let's look at some of your options and then consider how you decide which to select. Assume you are a generic staff manager (no particular function, but definitely not a line manager). You have the opportunity to recommend to your generic boss a structure for your function across the organization. The boss wants you to lay out all the options and recommend the one that would best meet the organization's needs. Here is a starting list of options. Read it and add a few of your own.

Structural options

1. Centralized function with all supporting staff located at headquarters, reporting directly to the Chief Executive Officer.

2. Centralized function, same as no. 1, but reporting to a line executive who reports to the CEO.

3. Centralized function, same as no. 1, but reporting to a staff executive who reports to the CEO.

4. Centralized function with all supporting staff reporting directly to the staff manager at headquarters, but many located in the field with no accountability to their customers in the field.

5. Same as no. 4, except that field staff are accountable to their customers secondarily—and primarily are accountable to their staff manager at headquarters.

6. The field staff report to both their functional manager at headquarters and the senior line manager at their field loca-

tion. They are responsible for serving each equally well and must balance this dual responsibility.

7. Staff management at headquarters performs in a support capacity to field staff, who are primarily responsible for serving their line customers. Field staff report to a senior line manager in the field and keep headquarters advised of their actions. Headquarters staff management collects field data, analyzes company trends, recommends company policy and procedure, coordinates the development of the field staff, and has related duties.

8. No staff management at headquarters, just some senior consultants reporting to a related staff function. These consultants bring their expertise to the field staff when requested. The field staffs around the company operate quite independently of each other with only occasional coordination. They are solely responsible to the line manager they report to; they operate as if the unit they serve were a small, independent company.

9. Same as no. 8, with no one in a staff capacity at headquarters.

10. No staff anywhere. All of this staff function is performed by the line organization as an integral part of the line job.

So here are ten options. What would you add?

Choosing a structure

I can help you in the choice by posing questions and offering my biases. Here is a long list containing both.

1. Tend toward more centrally controlled structures when your goals are:

   • To control the actions of others.

   • To offer unique services not available elsewhere.

   • To develop special skills for the future.

- To do research.

- To develop staff professionals.

- To reduce duplication of effort.

- To achieve economies of scale.

- To respond to urgent problems quickly.

- To feel important by having a lot of people reporting directly to you.

- To influence the top management of the organization.

2. Tend toward less centrally controlled structures when your goals are:

   - To emphasize service to field locations.

   - To build independence of talented field professionals.

   - To pursue goals not included in the centralized list.

3. Think of structure as evolving. You do not need to have the structure you want today—at least, not always. Figure out the ideal structure and move toward it over a few years rather than a few weeks.

4. Consider how other staff functions are structured in your corporation, how successful they are, and what you could learn from their success (or lack of success).

5. Consider what you most want to do in this staff function and where you could do this most effectively.

6. Know that changes in structure are quite costly in human energy—much more costly that most of us realize. There are few interventions in our organizational lives that disrupt us

as completely as having our jobs redefined in an organizational shuffle. Make major structural change only when the alternative promises to be significantly better than the status quo and worth the costs incurred in transition.

7. A decentralized organization with links between headquarters and the field requires building a supporting system to allow it to work. Roles at the various levels and locations become particularly important. Mechanisms that interface related staff—even though geographically distant—need to be developed and supported.

8. Sort out your stake in this structure as separate from the organization's stake. What do you want from this structure?

9. Who are the powerful people and how do you gain access to them? Your place in the structure affects your contact with them.

10. Do not structure your function just to handle today's problems. This puts you in a highly reactive stance and does not move you toward the future (you won't have time; you will be too focussed on today). Instead, build a structure that provides resources for dealing with the future, for implementing your strategy, and for taking care of ongoing responses to the needs of your line customers.

11. How often do you need to deal with the senior people in the organization? Occasional contact does not require a direct reporting relationship. How else might you access them besides reporting to them?

12. Restructuring generates a host of consequences as your new structure impacts others. Be prepared for the consequences—especially the negative reactions—since they will cost you much energy.

13. Centralize/decentralize is more of a power issue than a location issue. It is very possible to have your resources widely

distributed geographically and still have them report to you centrally. You will need to establish clear ways of working together.

14. When structuring, think about the abilities of the people you now have. A structure that makes all kinds of organizational sense will not work if your people's present abilities cannot support it.

15. Whether you inherit an old structure or are building a new one, begin thinking early about what structure would be appropriate. Even if no one will allow you to do anything about it right now, your advance thought prepares you to take up the opportunity when it comes along.

16. Centralized staff groups often abuse their privilege, not by intent so much as by location, power, and time. This is not to argue against centralized staff organizations. Instead it is to emphasize what can happen when you gather a group of like-functioned individuals together under one person. The visibility of these staff groups makes them easier to criticize than their decentralized counterparts hidden throughout the company. They will likely be criticized for being too large, too expensive, too slow, too specialized, too ivory-towered, too powerful, and too out of touch with the real world. Expect these criticisms as a natural consequence of the way you have structured yourself. And also know that they are true—or becoming true—at this moment. To have it otherwise requires constant vigilance.

17. Centralized staff groups should empower their counterparts in the field. Field professionals should feel more confident, better developed, more knowledgeable, more powerful, and more effective with their line customers because of their central support.

18. Who are your primary customers? What is the best structure to meet their needs? This brings a focus on output, results, and the product of staff effort rather than the tradi-

tional staff preoccupation with input, expertise, activity, and methodology—not a bad note on which to conclude these structural considerations.

19. The options for alternative structures are multiplied when you begin to think in terms of partial decentralization. What if you decentralized some of your work but not all of it? Or what if you decentralized all of your work to some parts of the organization but not to all parts of the organization?

20. Some aspects of structure seem important in managing your staff. The strong impetus toward staff specialization has encouraged us and our people to see their work as very unique—which, in fact, it is. This uniqueness deserves recognition and not necessarily through the structures we establish. My main concern is establishing a structure that is vertically deep and horizontally narrow. Too many staff departments end up stacking specialists three or four levels deep with supervisors having a span of control of two or three people. I think this comes from paying too much attention to our own staff business and not enough attention to the corporation's. Look at your organizational chart. If you find a predominance of three-on-one supervisory relationships rather than six-on-one, chances are you have too many working supervisors. If this is true through three levels of the structure, I would wonder whether one level of supervision could be eliminated to the advantage of departmental results, professional motivation, and your budget.

21. From a supervisory perspective, I have a large concern for the perceptions we are building in the heads of our professionals when we fit them into narrow boxes. We distance them from the reality of the working, sweating part of the corporation that pays their salaries. We reduce their professional flexibility as we encourage them to think more deeply about less. We limit our own ability to adapt to the changing corporate world that needs us for this today and something quite different tomorrow. When managing a group made up of individual contributors, I favor a flatter

organization.When managing a group made up of staff operations people, I favor less hierarchy, wider spans of control, and supervisors who spend most of their time supervising.

Leading with Confidence

✔ **Overview**

✔ **Dare to Risk**

✔ **Create Your Own Rewards**

✔ **Investment in Change**

✔ **More Power to You**

✔ **Positive Politics**

✔ **Solid Relationships**

Overview

The last section of the book explored a hierarchy starting with mission at the highest level and working down through systems and methods. My attempt was to proceed logically from those higher-order directions to the lower-order actions.

This section is a companion to the last. It is much less logical, not hierarchical and planful like the last. It is, however, just as important. We will be considering chapters on risk, reward, change, power, politics, and work relationships. These are often leading issues in our staff management struggles to get on top of our jobs. They each represent opportunity as well as anxiety; we are frequently both drawn to them and repelled by them. Important aspects of our organizational world, they guide us as we plan and pursue other more rational managerial behavior. They affect all of our actions.

Dare to Risk 12

W hat do you risk when you speak out on an issue in your organization? What is it that just might happen that causes you to get nervous, clutch, perspire, worry, lie awake, hesitate, fumble, or stutter? What are you putting on the line that you might lose? Here is a short risk list for you to choose from.

What do you stand to lose?

Job	Respect of others	Privileges
Praise	Boss's favor	Role
Authority	Affection of others	Image
Power	Salary increase	Respect
Neutrality	Political position	

It will vary somewhat from situation to situation, but for those of us who feel risk often, there is usually a pattern to the kind of personal concern that we have. We are usually trying to protect the same parts of our organizational and personal anatomy.

For example, one advertising manager has much difficulty risking because he is concerned that the people he works with will not like him. As a result, when risking even small disagreements with his associates, he laughs a great deal and tries to get them to smile or laugh with him. This gives him some assurance that they still like him as a person—at least that is why he does this. Not surprisingly, they are seldom even thinking about liking him as being an issue; they are more focussed on the idea he has put before them and wondering why he keeps joking and laughing and taking them off the subject. This behavior causes them to rather seriously draw him back to the point, and, of course, their seriousness tells him that they are not liking him, which causes him to try to get them to smile. Do you get the idea?

So what is at risk when you get nervous? What are you trying to protect? Understanding it will help you become more aware of what is happening while it is happening. The advertising manager described above knows well what he goes through to secure others' affection for him. When he was having significant difficulty dealing with his associates, he sought help from a consultant who called him and his associates together to look at performance. That meeting yielded the description of him you read in the last paragraph. He has since found other ways of assuring their liking for him and is now better able to make his points to them quite directly, unclouded by all his personal smoke. People say they now like working with him better and see him as more effective, even more likeable, in the work setting.

A risky process

How do you go about risking? Well, it's risky:

1. Identify situations in which you often feel at risk on the job.

2. Identify what the discomfort is; look for the pattern through many specific events at work (and outside work) and express your concerns by filling in the blanks of this sentence: "The risk is that if I _____(take this action)_____, then _____(this dire result)_____ will happen."

3. Figure out the worst possible thing that could happen as a result of taking this risk. For a moment, indulge your negative fantasy. Commonly we feel we will lose our jobs, we will be ostracized, we will be laughed at and rendered ineffective. Whatever it is, say it aloud to yourself.

4. Tell someone you trust who is outside this risky situation about the risk and what you fear. If you can, tell others. Ask them to tell you about something similar that has happened to them.

5. Tell a few people who are in the risky situation about your concerns. Get their reaction to them.

6. Compare their perspective on what is happening (or might happen) with your own. Notice how much or little their thoughts fit with your own.

7. If the fear is still working on you, do step 5 again with others from the risky work situation.

8. Decide on small possible actions you can take that represent different behavior for you in these risky situations. Draw on the ideas others have given you in doing this.

9. Try out your new, small, safe actions.

10. Check with others on how you are doing. Do they notice any differences? Often they will not notice your changes. They are so involved in their own lives that they don't see the significant small changes you have made, and they often did not even know you were fearful in the first place.

These words express rather concisely the importance of risk in staff management. These words are of course not limited to staff managers—though I do think they are particularly apt for us. Any staff function that wants to influence the direction of the larger organization necessarily must risk telling that organization what it ought to keep doing, what it ought to change, what it ought to stop doing. All of these actions require taking a position—defining who you are and where you stand—and that means risk. How do you know what your contribution is if you cannot identify it? What is happening differently because of the presence of your depart-

Contribution is in direct relationship to willingness to risk*

*An idea from Walt Mahler.

ment? What is your unique contribution? Making a difference requires risk.

Here is yet another perspective on risk. Think of a line manager whom you want to behave quite differently *and* are afraid to confront. Think not so much about all the little specific changes he would have to make, but more about the magnitude of change you would have him make. Got it? Next, think about how much risk that would be for him. In helping him to change, are you willing to risk as much as you would expect him to risk in the changing? Are you willing to risk as much as you would have him risk? If your answer is "yes," then you have important preparation for being helpful: you are willing to take significant action yourself and you have some sense of what that line manager might be facing as he considers changing. If your answer is "no," then I would suggest you lower your expectations of your customer so you ask no more of him than you would ask of yourself.

Risk and fear

"In the office in which I work there are five people of whom I am afraid. Each of these five people is afraid of four people (excluding overlaps), for a total of twenty, and each of these twenty people is afraid of six people, making a total of one hundred and twenty people who are feared by at least one person. Each of these one hundred and twenty people is afraid of the other one hundred and nineteen, and all of these one hundred and forty-five people are afraid of the twelve men at the top who helped found and build the company and now own and direct it."*

Most of us know what Heller is talking about. We find ourselves at risk and hesitating to move forward. We are afraid of what might happen or afraid that something has happened that will cause us to lose something valuable to us. There is the distinct possibility that we have risked more than we intended, or that we may be called upon to choose one goal over another, or that our actions may not work out in the way we intended. You know what you see as the risks of working in your organization better than anyone else.

*Joseph Heller, *Something Happened* (New York: Ballentine Books, 1975), p. 9.

Paradoxically, the best way to get around these fears is frequently by going through them. Instead of moving away from our darker corners, moving toward them and bringing them out into the light can help. By looking at what we are afraid of, we can understand our fears better. We can anticipate situations in which a fear might arise and also avoid situations that we cannot handle as well as we would like because of our fears.

Here is another way to clarifying what your risks and responsibilities are:

Sorting risk responsibilities

1. Picture an executive, above your boss's level, whom you find it particularly risky to deal with.

2. Think about an important issue that you would like to put before that person.

3. Next imagine yourself putting the issue before this person. How do you feel? Scribble down all the thoughts and feelings you would expect to have at that moment.

4. Now, how would you like to feel at that moment? Scribble down all those thoughts and feelings, too.

5. Compare the two lists: the length of the lists, the types of thoughts and feelings on each, the direction of the change from one list to the other, the overlap between the lists.

6. Now ask yourself what the executive does that causes you to feel as you do when you put the issue before her—rather than how you would like to feel. Write these points down, noting everything you can that contributes significantly to how you feel.

7. Write down everything *you* do that causes you to feel other than the way you would like to at this difficult moment. What do you do that gets in the way of your better feelings about yourself?

8. If this list is hard to make, chances are you are in one of these siutations:

- You are not doing anything that causes you to feel bad— it's all the other guy's fault.

- You just haven't thought about it this way before and it takes a while to get on that wave length.

- You have thought about it and know this path leads nowhere because even if you accept some responsibility, the other person still can control how you feel.

In one way or another, all the alternatives offered above ask you to think about your responsibility for feeling differently from what you would like about an encounter with a difficult executive. No, it isn't always your fault. No, I am not saying we deserve everything we get. Yes, I am saying that when it comes to thinking about changing behaviors, it is damned difficult to change someone else. So let's start where it is most practical—with the person we have the most control over, with the individual we are most invested in. Let's start with ourselves. For many, this is not a new thought. For some, turning the spotlight on themselves, on their own behavior, is blinding and temporarily immobilizing.

What is the worst thing that could possibly happen?

We considered that question earlier, and I am returning to it now because it seems so appropriate in light of the way we often discuss the risks of living in a large organization. So often that question evokes this response: "I could be fired!"

If individuals were fired even one-tenth as often as that fear crosses the minds of this country's threatened staff managers, there would be damned few of us on the job today. The response contains more bravado than truth. It evokes images of staff managers laying their jobs on the line in the cause of some higher staff value or, perhaps more accurately, talking bravely about how they almost laid their jobs on the line and withdrew at the last minute in the cause of organizational survival. And their peers, over a drink after work, supported them—at least until the harrowing story was finished and there was time for the listener to tell her equally harrowing tale.

The truth is that losing your job is *not* the worst thing that could ever happen for most of us. It is just what we talk about to boisterously cover our more threatened selves. Worse than losing a job is *keeping* a job in which you are not respected, or not listened to, or not consulted, or not liked, or not influential, or . . . You name it; it's your fear. Being clear on what it is helps you as you work with others because you are better able to sort the difference between what is happening to you on the outside and what you are doing to yourself on the inside.

As devoted staff professionals we have chosen positions that give others some apparent power over us. Our devotion to our work often puts us in vulnerable positions with the customers we serve: they can accept or reject our work; they can speak well or poorly of us to those we work with; and they can choose to seek or avoid assistance from us. This is where professional vulnerability lies for many of us. We know (or strongly suspect) that we won't be fired, but what if we can't ply our staff trade? That is the larger risk.

Create Your Own Rewards

13

For many of us, gaining the rewards available in staff management requires a significant refocussing of our work and our perspective. It is not the same as the work we had before we became a manager. We all know that, and too many of us continue to pursue the satisfactions available to us as individual contributors—or long for those good old days. Pursuing and longing will not do it. Renouncing is probably a better word. There are new rewards available to us, but they are not extensions of what we did before we took on this departmental responsibility.

As individual contributors, we invested years in completion of projects, on time, to the satisfaction of our supervisor and to the praise of our professional peers, honing our technical skills, in control of our efforts and outcomes, working alone, working in task forces, being the expert, seeing the results of our efforts, getting feedback through our work, drawing on the guidance of others. Well, perhaps it was not quite that glorious, but you know what I mean. All of the above sources of satisfaction are much more plentiful at the individual contributor level than they are at the staff management level. Maybe it shouldn't be that way, but it is. Partly it is a function of the organizational pyramid—there are just fewer people at your level and far fewer at your boss's level. You can see that many of the sources of satisfaction are cut into by having fewer people around you invested in what you do.

Finding rewards

So you are more alone with more responsibility than you have ever had before. *This* is rewarding??? Finding rewards in this job requires looking in quite a different place and too often there is no one there to tell you where to look, whether you are "getting hot" or "getting cold"—as we used to say in a childhood game. Here are some clues to finding rewards:

- Take your eye off the ball and look at the field.

- Pursue vision, mission, philosophy, values, and strategy rather than this month's project. See the forest, not the trees (or the leaves).

- Coach, do not play—and find real satisfaction in the sidelines role.

- Direct the function, not the project.

- Strategize your function's influence on corporate direction rather than convince one customer.

- See others learn, develop, and succeed; do not do it all yourself.

- Coordinate your efforts with other staff managers; do not compete with them.

- See an important staff function mature toward its mission to the benefit of the organization it serves.

- Become a respected member of the management team.

- Influence long-term management decisions.

- See what your department is doing in relation to what similar departments in other organizations are doing.

Many of the above rewards are available to all managers, line and staff. The rewards more unique to you have to do with your function's influence on the larger organization and its objectives. You have that special authority for your functional area that no one else has. Your boss has others like you reporting to him who have their own unique function. But you are Mr. Traffic or Ms. Accounts Receivable or Miss Public Relations or Mrs. Safety for this organization. Your line counterparts do not have this same kind of uniqueness. They are usually unique in the geographic area (Northern Regional Manager) or facility (Peoria Plant) that they head up. And there is usually also a Southern Region and a Dallas Plant where there is somebody else with a job very much like theirs. Nobody else has a job like yours in this organization.

Your rewards are dependent on your recognition of this special-ness. You need to recognize it and capitalize on it. Use this oppor-tunity to show the organization the unique contribution your staff department can make in moving the larger organization toward its objectives. Don't wait silently for their recognition. Show them what your department can do; educate them on the value of your work. Results lead to more of the recognition you want from your customers, your peers, your staff, and yourself.

Never enough reward

You are unlikely to get the kind of appreciation for your work that you would like to get from line management. Let's put it this way: don't stay in this work if you must be appreciated on your own terms for what you do.

This could imply that our line customers are hard-nosed, uncar-ing bastards. We all know some who are, but line management has no monopoly on this type of person—look around other staff departments and (heaven forbid!) your own. In large organizations we generally come up short when it comes to bestowing appreciation on our workers, be they hourly, supervisory, professional, or managerial. So what's a poor and needy staff manager to do?

Look to ourselves for appreciation, confirmation, affirmation, celebration, and all those other "-ations" we want so much. See recognition from others as a bonus, the frosting on the cake rather than the cake itself. We provide our own best recognition. We know what we want; it's time to give it to ourselves! We also know when we deserve it and when we don't.

Which reminds me, why is it that at those times when you do get recognition from line management, it often misses the mark? "He told me he really liked the three-ring binder design, but he didn't mention what's inside!" See? When they do it, they often do it "wrong"—wrong in the sense that it does not meet the recognition needs we have. We could have written their lines much better and delivered them more sincerely and enthusiastically, too!

The fact is that they do not know how to recognize us on our own terms because they do not know what "our own terms" are. They would have to be there with us and our subordinates, doing the work, to know how much praise we deserve. The other side of this is that we cannot give them adequate recognition, either—for the same reasons. So many of us must turn to ourselves or our own kind to get the strokes and professional appreciation we deserve.

Praise needed breeds dependence

That means the praisor has power over the praisee. The truth of that is probably more obvious when it comes to criticism—you know the power you give the criticizer. The trick is to somehow appreciate that special recognition you get and at the same time not need it in a dependent way. Look to yourself first to recognize what you do; derive your primary satisfaction from meeting your own internal standards. Supplement that satisfaction with what you receive from others. In more trying times, when others are not there to give the recognition and support, you will be stronger for having depended on yourself in the good times.

T here are rewards for which you have to put your tail on the line. And putting it there doesn't assure that you will get the reward you are seeking (internal or external). In fact, you might not emerge from the scrimmage intact. It just may not be worth it. You have considered the risk and you have decided. Reconsideration of those risks is a healthy thing for a staff manager to do periodically. Here are steps for reconsidering those risks:

Reconsidering risk and reward

1. Start that reconsideration with an assessment of how rewarding your job is to you lately. What does it give you for all that you put into it? How important are those rewards to you? Where do those rewards come from? Your boss? You employees? Your customers? Your peers? Your top management? Yourself? How dependent/independent do these rewards make you on others? If you had to look just to the rewards that you get from yourself, how satisfying would this job be?

2. *If* you want to change the rewards you get from this job, how would you change them? *If* you could, what would you alter? How would these fantasized changes affect your dependence on/independence from others?

3. *If* you were to pursue those rewards, what kinds of actions would be required of you that are different from those you are taking now? Put aside the risks for a moment and just think about what you would have to do to get some of those positive consequences you are dreaming about. Imagine yourself in situations that would possibly yield those positive results. Imagine what you would be doing.

Create Your Own Rewards 131

4. What would be the risk of doing it, of going after the reward, of acting to get the work satisfaction you are seeking? What are you risking? How could it hurt you? Others? How big a risk is it? And what are the chances of success? Would it be worth it?

The above exercise is intended as constructive fantasy rather than a prescription for how to handle your particular reality. It is a short fantasy you can put beside those other less-guided imaginings you have when faced with the possibilities of risk and reward. You may have confirmed what you already know. Your understanding of your job's risks and rewards—and your response to them—is quite thorough. Fine.

My hope was to stimulate new thought, new perspectives on what you now do, and your responsibilities within what you do. If you are pleased with what is happening now in your staff management work life and if you are getting the rewards you want, then I suggest you continue along your present course. If, on the other hand, there are significant empty spots in your staff management life; if you are far from getting what you want, then prepare yourself to change *something*—because something isn't working to your advantage. If you were playing tennis and losing (and cared), you probably would not stick with your same playing strategy. So it is with your staff management game: change your strategy when this one isn't yielding the rewards you want.

Investment in Change 14

Staff departments seem to have a big investment in change. We are always looking for ways to help our customers do their jobs even better than they do them now. And we are frequently disappointed in the changes we see. I am certain that you could come up with three to five rather profound changes you would like to see take place in your organization—if you only had the magic wand. This chapter lists a number of ideas on bringing about change in others and in yourself.

Do not overestimate your ability to bring about change—or underestimate the organization's ability to maintain itself without chaning. When we are less experienced in organizational life, steeped in our professional ideals, naivete about how to bring about change prevails. Our presumptions often lie at the

It isn't easy. . .

extremes: "This organization will never change (despair, despair)"; or "If they just changed this one policy, it would fix everything! (oh joy, oh joy)." Both extremes do happen, but most organizational change falls between these poles.

Why rapid change seldom work

For the moment, assume the organization can be changed as quickly as you would like. Now, what is to prevent someone else from coming along and changing it again tomorrow? That is one of the down sides of fast organizational change that we often do not stop to imagine. The same inclinations, abilities, or assumptions that allowed my "good" change to happen so rapidly are also available to the next change-maker who comes along.

Respect the organization

A lot of miles are on this old organization you want to change. A lot of people are invested in it. A lot of work has gone into making it what it is today. If you don't respect that now, you soon will as you try to change what is happening—perhaps a grudging respect, but respect nevertheless. A change-maker who doesn't respect the organization being changed will find many organizational forces lined up against the change and will have to deal with that organization's defensive posture throughout the change effort. Change is possible without respect, but it ain't easy.

This is the hardest part. Coming up with the ideas for change and the plan for implementation, even the management approvals—all this is easy in a major change effort when compared to implementing the change and making it an established part of "how we do business around here." In the long run the change must maintain itself without continual energy transfusions from you. It must move ahead on its own momentum. Others must see that it happens because they both understand it and support its happening. For important change, reaching this point does not take days or weeks; it takes months or years. Now . . . what are you prepared to give?

So prepare to endure . . . to persevere . . . to hold the line

At the risk of sounding anti-innovation, I'll say we have too many "idea persons" in staff departments and not enough persistent and creative implementers. Many of us who are very good at coming up with the new ideas are sorely needed in the implementation stage—when we want to go off to do other creative things. One definition of innovation has to do with the combination of creative imagination and application, resulting in innovation in its most practical sense. That is what we need in staff functions: more innovation over the long term; less creativity over the short term.

"I'm an idea person . . . somebody else can carry it out better than I"

Do not fool yourself. There is somebody else in that very job right now, and she probably said the same thing before moving to that position. Committing to acting tomorrow is often a lie—or at least should be dealt with as a lie. Seeing it as such allows you to begin to explore other opportunities today. Tomorrow will never come, and even if it did, you would not be the person you are today (as the person filling the job you want can testify).

"When I get the job I want, *then* I'll make the changes . . ."

I am reminded of the employee we all know who is saving for retirement. Not just money, but experiences, growth, opportunity, everything. Too often when retirement arrives, the employee has saved so long, so many years, that he doesn't know how to spend. He has trained himself not to spend for years and cannot simply untrain himself at the instant he receives the gold watch. This can happen to you and me as we rationalize our need not to take action just yet. Instead we would do better to assume we are going to act and decide what would work best. Assume that, if you establish a pattern of waiting to act, over the years you will forget what it is you were waiting to do.

An idea whose time has come

Many ideas—including many of yours—are waiting for the time when they will be seen as practical. Timing is a larger factor in acceptance of ideas than their basic worthiness. There is probably a "right time" for most every idea, but that time is seldom now. Only a few ideas are apropos of this moment in time; finding them now is what is difficult. Ideas don't age. Old ideas, new ideas—to a situation demanding solution, when the idea was originally conceived is much less important than whether it can help solve this problem now. So it didn't work three years ago. What has that got to do with right now? Don't fail to put forth an idea because it has been proposed before. Let present need be your guide, not history.

Change in a changing organization

One of the biggest problems I experienced as a staff manager was getting the organization to hold still long enough for my staff group to fully diagnose a problem, come up with a solution that the line supports, implement it, support it long enough that it begins to maintain itself, and measure the results of this intervention. It's like trying to give a spoonful of medicine to a screaming, struggling, sick child who won't hold still long enough for you to get a full tablespoon in its mouth. The medicine ends up everywhere but where it ought to be; the child sees the cure as worse than the illness; and you end up using methods that don't seem in keeping with the child's ill health. And in the end, you often wonder whether the child might have gotten better anyway, without the help of modern medicine.

Let's face it, the organization is not going to hold still. And its movement is not in protest against the "medicine" you are attempting to administer. No, most of the movement comes about just because the organization is trying to adapt to what is happening within and without itself. An organization is like an organism in its need to respond to the internal and external pressures it feels.

Part of the problem we experience as we attempt to change the organization is that it is already changing—and it's not waiting for us. From this perspective, organizational change is less being a traffic cop who stands out in front and detours the organization in some new direction and more being a cowpoke who throws a saddle on a moving horse as it goes by, cinches it as tight as he can under the circumstances, and holds on for dear life a *long* time before attempting to influence the beast. To the extent we think of the organization as a more static structure, we are bound to be surprised. Our models and methods for bringing about change must recognize the state of flux that is the organization.

I ronically, one of the larger reasons for organizational change comes out of success. Just when you find that line executive who supports your functions in the way you like, she gets promoted and you have to start over with her successor. Or just when you develop a subordinate to the point where he can operate well on his own, he accepts a job with another organization and you must start over. Or just when a project or system you instituted in one division begins to establish itself, the rest of the company

The perils of success

gets hot on the early returns and insists that you take your good ideas company-wide, and you have to dilute your efforts in the first division. Each of these examples demonstrates that success can throw your change efforts off track and, from that perspective, isn't always a blessing.

Change and relationships

As we work to bring about change, we'd better attend to the relationships we are establishing with our customers. We want to influence them in a way that also enhances the relationship.* Think about it . . . It is more uniquely our situation than the line's that we must pay attention to both what we want people to do and how we get them to do it. It has to do with the dependent nature of our role and the independence of theirs. So the way that we work with them often determines not only how but whether they will use us.

Helping bring about change while improving your relationship with your customers requires paying attention to what is happening in some new ways. You take in new data; you measure what is happening against different scales; you behave differently. Consider the differences between these two expected outcomes for a meeting: "By the end of the meeting I want him to let us modify the data retrieval system currently used by his department." As contrasted with "I hope that by the end of the meeting he will be looking forward to our help on the data retrieval system, and to have expressed his appreciation for our help on his problem." These two expected outcomes are different enough to require quite different behaviors. The second includes enhancement of the relationship as one of the primary objectives of the meeting while the first, though not precluding it, does not emphasize the quality of the relationship. It allows for all kinds of behavior that would conflict with the relationship objective.

*I am indebted to Boyce Appel for this helpful perspective.

More Power to You

15

" . . . But I'm only staff." You see the words. Can you hear them, too? What do they sound like? What are the feelings behind them? I hear fear and resignation and anger. And I don't like it. I was talking with another consultant about this, and he said, "It drives me bananas! This self-imposed impotence expressed by some staff managers is overwhelming." How can a manager who regularly pleads "I'm only staff . . ." be effective? And how can he be so blind to what that mental framework prevents him from doing?

The reality is that most staff positions come with less formal power assigned to them, and formal power is important. There are many other sources of power to draw upon—if we can move ourselves out of the perspective of being "only staff."

Here are some questions that you may have struggled with:

• How do you get things accomplished without formal power?

• How do you acquire eligibility to put forth ideas and be heard?

• How do you get others to see staff's importance to the line?

- What do you want to do that you cannot now do because you lack the power?

- What power do you now have? Where does it come from?

- How could you use the power you now have more effectively?

- How do you become a part of "what's happening" in your organization?

The answers are not easy, but putting positive energy into the questions usually yields alternative approaches that empower us more than griping does. Read this chapter and then return to the above questions. I'll bet you will have some new answers.

Exceeding our limits

There are so many things that a staff manager cannot do. Ask us and we'll tell you. I have spoken of many of those things in this book. It is time to challenge those limits.

Let's tackle the big one first—authority. The one we can't have. This last phrase calls up an important distinction: "can't have" versus "shouldn't have." Let's withhold judgment for the time being on how much authority goes with being a staff manager and look at what is possible. As we look across the corporate experience, we can see that anything is possible. Comptrollers have taken over companies. Lawyers have determined organizational directions. Human resource vice-presidents have become a critical influence on the management committee. But not in your company, you say. True, if you say so, but we are not talking about your company right now; we are talking about what has happened and can happen—what is possible.

And we are not discussing how these staff executives moved to their authority, or whether they ought to be there, or how effectively they are doing the job, or how long they will last. Our sole emphasis at this moment is whether it can be done—and it has been done repeatedly. To say otherwise is to accept a lie. It has been done! That is the truth!

The fact that somebody has done it, in fact many somebodies have done it, is experience and makes us quite different from the first staff manager who attempted to move into a position of authority. We are not the first woman to ever run a marathon facing an athletic world that said women could never run that far. We are not the men who first assaulted the four-minute-mile barrier. No, we are staff managers exploring the authority we can have in an organization. And as we look around at what other staff managers have done, we can find many who have taken on roles of great authority and power. We cannot say that it will never be done or that it cannot be done.

We can say, "I have not done it." Or "I don't think I should do it." Or "I don't believe I could do it." Or "I don't want to do it." Or "I don't know how to do it." These are statements of personal responsibility. They each reflect an awareness of where I stand in relation to authority in my situation. These statements do not use what others have done or not done to support or excuse my actions. These are mature statements.

They are to be contrasted with: "It's wrong for a staff manager to participate in line decisions." Or "Nobody in a staff position around here could ever do that." Or "What can we do about it? We're only staff." Or "They would never let us get involved." These statements assign responsibility for our actions to some higher rule, or authority, or underlying assumption. The "I" statements are missing, the personal responsibility is not evident. Notice the difference between the two sets of statements. Put aside your judgments about the truth of any of the statements and focus on the difference between saying "I will not . . ." and "They won't let us . . ."

"They won't . . ." vs. "I haven't . . .

The perspective is entirely different, isn't it? "I" statements allow me to be in control; I am choosing what I will do and I am aware of my choice. "They" statements assume their power and my subordinance to it. "They" statements put the focus outside myself and make me dependent on them. Generalizations ("Staff managers never . . .") also take the focus off me and move it to the amorphous "they." This not only misses the point, but weakens us in relation to the point. It is a view that portrays us as smaller, less important, less responsible, and not in charge. I am hammering away at a point I have already made. But the point is so important to my personal and staff management effectiveness that I do not want to risk minimizing it.

Out there vs. in here

Another slant has to do with change. Staff managers frequently ask what they can do to change and to become more effective. What course can I take? What book should I read? What are the three steps I need to follow? What are the right answers? All of these questions reflect a perspective that might be expressed as "There is something out there that I need to learn. If I could find that, I would be more successful. The right answer is out there somewhere." This approach has led many of us on fruitful searches for personal and professional growth and hasn't yielded many absolute answers.

Another approach, reflecting another perspective, involves an internal search. It might be expressed in this way: "There are some things about myself that I do not fully appreciate. When I allow myself to move in the directions dictated by my inner self, I feel more confident and responsible. There are answers within me." This approach has also led many of us to personal and professional growth—and it is only one approach.

Notice how the "answers are out there somewhere" approach ties to the they-are-responsible statements we were discussing earlier. It is easy to imagine a staff manager saying to himself both "They would never let us . . ." and "The right answer is out there somewhere." Notice the external focus of both these statements. Notice the dependence that the statements assume. I end up being a staff manager seeking answers in a world that somebody else controls.

Now notice how the process of looking into yourself for knowledge ties to the "I am responsible" statements we were discussing earlier. It's easy to imagine a staff manager saying to herself both "I am choosing not to . . ." and "There are answers within me." Notice the internal focus of both these statements. Notice the independence that the statements assume. I am a staff manager taking personal responsbility for my actions and growth.

The role you perform is a function of both the power that comes with your position and the power that comes with the way you choose to perform within your position. Power—formal and informal—is critical to the shaping of your staff role. Other words that relate to the same thing include authority, control, freedom, responsibility, and accountability. Each of them has formal and informal components, balanced to define your role.

Power through role

Too many of us accept our staff role as given, thinking of the more formal definition of what we are to do. Often not even the formal role is a given—if "given" means fixed and immutable. As actors within the role we are strong influencers of how the role is formally defined. If anybody is going to redefine it—or recommend redefinition—it will likely be us. Yes, when we move into our staff management job, there is a rather fixed formal authority that accompanies the position and that has profound impact on what we will do within this position. And this is not all there is to it.

Part of the given in the staff management role is that no matter what, our formal authority is limited by the fact that we are in a staff, not a line, position. No matter how much formal authority we can pull together, it still isn't much when compared to our line customers. Usually our most powerful formal authority is limited to our functional realm and obviously at the discretion of senior line management who delegated our authority to us in the first place. Here is what I suggest you do about your formal authority:

1. *Find out what it is.* What is written about it, said about it, and universally agreed to? Make certain that you understand this.

2. *Find out how it is working.* Do an authority audit. Does everyone know how they should work with your department? What parts of the company are doing this particularly well? Where do you have regular problems? In this audit, start with your own staff and use their data to help guide you in deciding which of your customers to talk with.

3. *Describe the formal authority you would like to have in order to carry out your function particularly well.* Consider the functional areas you would like to have under your authority. Consider what decisions you would like to make and how you would like to involve others. Consider how you would like to distribute authority within your department.

4. *Compare and contrast the authority you have, your authority audit, and the formal authority you would like to have.* Note where you have what you want and where you have important gaps. Decide which gaps are most important to close, and figure out ways to close them. Be patient; don't try to change everything overnight. Instead think more strategically about how you could alter your formal authority through time. During this step, also give significant thought to the implications of your actions for your customers. Watch out for actions that are beneficial to you but hurt the organization. One of the more obvious places you can redistribute authority is within your own department. Through delegation, you can move authority and responsibility downward in your staff hierarchy.

5. *Act.* Take your first steps toward altering your formal authority. Your formal authority is obviously related to your boss's, so there is no way to leave the boss out of the process. Earlier

involvement often gives you more information and secures commitment through boss participation. At the same time, you have to be aware of the potential threat to bosses who see their authority as being undermined as you build your own.

6. *Check.* When you make these formal shifts, how are they working? Monitor the differences they make.

Here are some other thoughts about power for you to consider:

Perspectives on power

1. *Power envy.* Many of us in staff roles suffer from "power envy" as we look at what our line customers have that we don't have. "He can do that because he's got approval authority and I don't." "I wish I had her job. If I did, I'd act a lot differently." "They can get away with anything as long as they have the CEO behind them." How much of our energy do we spend envying what line managers have? How much do we waste decrying what we lack? How often do we give up, saying we can't do it because we don't have it? And how much power do we gain through our envying of others?

We do not build our own power and esteem by proclaiming somebody else's. We need to examine ourselves, see how we are made up, see what we have to offer, and quit judging our value entirely by line standards. Listen to this statement and ask yourself whether this is the way to be powerful: "The line people in our organization have all the power . . . We staff people can't do anything . . . It's no use trying to change them because they don't have to listen to us if they don't want to." If you were to say that, or believe that, what kind of power position does that put you in? How do you end up feeling about your role, your effectiveness? If that's the way you feel about your job, you'd better have a damned compelling outside reason for staying there. (Maybe you have four kids in college, so you can't afford to leave for three years. Or your organization has a generous medical plan, you are quite ill, and you would be uninsurable elsewhere.) There are a few grave reasons that could allow a competent staff manager to stick with an organization while holding the perspective quoted above.

2. *Absence makes the heart grow fonder.* It is the same way with the power of authority. Our shortage of formal power causes us to accentuate its importance. Oh, there are so many things I could do—if I only had power. For some of us, giving expression to this notion gives us the freedom not to act, the excuse for not doing anything. It is as if recognizing our self-defined sorry state absolves us from doing anything about it.

3. *The grass is brown on both sides of the fence.* Our power fantasies cause us to imagine much about the power that others have—especially line managers. In fact, they seldom have as much as we think they do. Or, put another way, much of what they do have is because we think they have it. We give it to them through perceiving them as powerful. Other people do the same things to us. They give us power or take it away from us based on what kind and amount of power they think we have. So much of power is in perception: self-perception and others' perceptions of us.

4. *If you think you are powerful, you are.* * Believing in your own ability to get what you want is enough to move you to actions you would not even consider if you held a weaker view of yourself. The roots of power go deeper than simply belief, but belief in yourself is critical to drawing most effectively on the powers you have available.

5. *If others think you are powerful, you are.* Believing in your ability to get what you want is enough to move others to actions they would not have considered if they held weaker views of you. Certainly your power in relation to them is not rooted only in belief, but, again, it helps.

6. *Power is not authority, authority is a power.* Power is getting what you want. Formal, organizationally backed authority

*Herb Cohen is eloquent on this subject.

is one way of doing that. It is not the only way and often not the best way. Staff managers who play the formal authority game find out quickly that they lose. Some of us sit around lamenting those losses while others of us are moving forward on the strength of other powers we have in the organization.

Wat powers do we have that line managers lack? You say you have never thought about that? Well, consider this short list; see how many fit you; and add one or two if you can.

Special staff powers

1. Staff managers have the power of perspective, to move around, nose around, look into all parts of the organization. The staff responsiblities that cause them to serve the whole organization also allow them to know about the whole organization. Line managers are narrowed to working within their own departments and as a result do not have legitimate access to the whole organization.

2. Staff managers develop skills that are useful in many organizations. For many of us, our professional loyalty is at least as strong as our organization loyalty. Though we are not working here with the intent of leaving or threatening to leave, that option is available to us—and more readily available to us than to many of our line counterparts. Many of us are just moving through this organization on our way to another higher-level job in the same profession but another company. Overall, more of us do this in staff work than in line work. So what power resides with us? More options. The power to leave and go elsewhere brings with it the power to be more effective here by doing our best work. We have to worry less about compromising our professional standards because we know we have the option of going somewhere else. And more of us have more options than our line counterparts.

3. Our jobs are not as readily defined, understood, and measured as line jobs. With that comes the opportunity to define our jobs that most line managers could only pray for. Their jobs are much more defined by the product, the line, the system, the territory than are ours. If we choose to, many of us can mold our jobs to what we want them to be and what the organization needs.

4. Many staff managers operate in a much longer time frame than line managers. The line suffers from being responsible for the bottom line. They must deliver the numbers *today*. This narrows their perspective on the organizational world, which is power-limiting when a broader and longer-range perspective is called for. We have the advantage of being in jobs that are not as easily measured—and not as immediately measured—allowing us to step back from our work more easily than managers on the line side. This perspective is available to more staff than line people. Whether we believe it or use it is another matter.

What is your reaction? Do you feel like adding to my list or throwing it away? Does it give you ideas or does it miss the point? Your reactions may say something about the power you have and want in your organization.

It's got to be in your heart

Something that is more important to you than salary, position, status, privilege . . . something that nobody can touch with their external rewards, promises of comfort, fringe benefits . . . something that remains strong during times of trial, punishment, or threat. That something is a clear sense of the kind of staff management professional you know you can be. It is much more than a job description. It is more like a mission or, on an individual basis, a vocation. It is a set of principles, a professional philosophy, a vision of potential that is nurtured through regular reflection. It provokes an emotional response similar to patriotism. You seek it out in what you read, and it does not suffer through repetition; it grows. You seek it out in your professional friends and especially value it in those whose work is similar to your own. You can identify it in those who are devoted to their work. Though "devoted" in the religious sense does sound a bit heavy, I doubt that it is when you consider how much energy we give to our work. This is where the real power is.

Positive Politics — 16

When you read the word "politics," what thoughts and feelings do you have? Corporate politics, company politics, departmental politics, organizational politics—our modifiers may differ, but the reality doesn't. Politics are part of the way a large organization operates. The thoughts and feelings you conjured up a moment ago are very important to how you deal with the political realities of your organization.

Did those thoughts and feelings add up to a generally negative total? If so, then this section is for you. The distaste you have for the politics of organizational life is based in stories and experience— and if I were with you right now, you could tell me a story or two that gives strong support for your position. I believe that because so many of us have experienced the down side of someone else's political moves. Hold those thoughts in abeyance for a few minutes while you read a few words about other aspects of politics in organizations.

Politics are real—and essential

Politics are not basically good or bad; they are to do with as we will. Their goodness or badness flows from the intent and the impact of our political actions. Politics are the basis of trust and distrust, loyalty and undermining, giving and withholding, contacting and avoiding. Without the formal and informal political systems that exist in your organization, it would come to a halt. Or perhaps because of the formal and informal political systems, it *has* come to a halt. Either case demonstrates the power and importance of politics in your organization.

Eliminating politics would mean eliminating the advance warning you get from an associate in another department—which she is not really supposed to give you. It would mean not being able to line up support for a proposal before an upcoming management meeting. It would mean no more chats with your boss's boss's boss about the direction of the department and his views of your possible role in that. Whether you are on the receiving end of these political benefits or not, you can imagine how each of them can help the organization and its members function more effectively. Keep these tips in mind:

- Acknowledge the reality of politics.

- Accept that they are essential and will not disappear.

- Begin to understand them.

- Recognize that you are a part of the politics.

- Act within this political framework in knowledgeable ways.

Years ago, I moved from one corporation to another in a way that significantly affected my political perspective. Before the move, I was a high-level individual staff contributor working on projects in a number of company subsidiaries. My emphasis was on achievement, completion of projects with quality results, time, and client satisfaction. After the move, I was the director of a corporate staff department, with others reporting to me, and responsible for the long-term direction of my function within the corporation. The individual contributors (my old position) now reported to people who reported to me. I hope you can see the great difference between the two positions.

In my new position I tried to apply the abilities that had worked so well in my previous job. I worked hard on projects—often as an individual contributor rather than a manager—and attempted to measure my success based on project achievement. Some of that worked, but there was something important missing, and it had to do with organizational politics. I was avoiding them like the plague! The more I avoided politics, the less I knew about what was going on in the political realms that were so important to that company's direction. Knowing less about what is happening is not the way to become influential; it is not the way that leads to sound management decisions.

Experience, and some wise consultation, convinced me to begin to move toward the political arena so I could understand it better and become more effective as a staff manager. Yes, moving toward it does mean risking "catching the disease" that I had seen in others. Yes, it does mean possibly losing perspective on what I held as important and being seduced by the political system. But moving toward understanding the politics of that organization made it more likely that I could influence its direction. And that I could influence the politics themselves by modeling behavior that supported my kind of politics.

While some of us avoid organizational politics, others of us exult in them to the point of finding our basic meaning there. We become preoccupied with the way you get things done, who's influential and who isn't, whose star is on the rise vs. whose is falling, what it is politic to say or avoid. Overindulgence in the process of getting things done results in far more energy being spent on thinking and observing than on action. At this political extreme a staff department can be immobilized as it waits for the right political moment. In contrast, a staff department can be destroyed by acting in ignorance of politics.

Staff functions as political breeding grounds

Talking the language

One indicator of political naivete on the part of a staff department is the language they use to communicate with others in the organization. As you listen to or read what your staff puts out, does it speak to the perspective of the intended reader or listener? Is it said in their language, considerate of their perspective, or is it loaded with the esoteric, distance-building staff jargon that many of us are so fond of? Ask one of your clients about how you communicate with him. Or consider the subject at a staff meeting.

There are words quite appropriate to a staff meeting or a professional society conference that should never escape our lips, our pens, or our keyboards in polite company ("polite company" meaning anyone outside the department or the profession). You know the jargon and the acronyms that are so prevalent in our staff conversations. The problem is that some of us forget when we are speaking our staff dialects. I suspect that both you and I pump out considerable verbal garbage that serves primarily to distance us from our customers.

"My kind of politics"

That phrase comes close to the heart of a distinction I was trying to make earlier: it's not that we don't like politics, it's that we want the political processes to happen in certain ways—which are generally healthy, clean, and other equally hygenic adjectives. Let's not fool ourselves. We are not going to be very effective as staff managers if we ignore the politics of the organization. Since politics is at least in part knowing how to work with others around you to get things done, we'd better pay attention if we want to accomplish something.

Solid Relationships 17

Building a balanced relationship where mutual power is recognized and shared is not easy. Those of us who are dependent on our line customers and bosses have to strengthen ourselves. Look at the progress we can make as moving through four stages: dependence, counterdependence, independence, and interdependence. This model comes from the field of interpersonal relationships and seems to have application to what we go through as staff managers. The order of the stages is not accidental, though it might not fit exactly with your experience. Many of us work through our relationships with line managers in just this order; others of us manage to cover the first three stages somehow before reaching interdependence but not the order listed above. To be truly interdependent, we have to have resolved the issues that exist in the three earlier stages. Let's look at each of the stages in terms of how the staff manager works with upper management. As we do this, know that the same four stages can be applied to your work with peers, customers, or your own staff.

Four stages

Dependence

In its pure form, the dependent role includes the staff manager willingly acknowledging—perhaps even extolling the virtues of—the essentially subordinate and less important aspects of the staff role. The whole bearing of this staff manager is affected by this honest perception. In its more positive forms, it is akin to being a management valet, here to know, love, and serve the master. There is no question about who has the power in this relationship. And there is no question about whether it can work; it can. It may best meet the needs of the situation, the line, and staff managers involved.

In its more negative forms, there is a lot of pretending involved. The staff manager in question pretends to respect line management when in fact she only respects the power of the position—"fears" might be a better word than "respects." The staff manager feels "one down" and doesn't see a constructive way out of the situation. The result is often destructive to organizational performance and to the staff manager. The personal destructiveness may be in the form of getting eaten up inside from all of the pretending the situation seems to require. More overtly, it may be the hurt that is felt when actions taken with the intent of changing the dependent relationship end up shoving the staff manager even more clearly, and unbearably, into the dependent position—as when a staff manager speaks up "inappropriately" and the line management reminds her that this is not her role (read "place").

Counter-dependence

Moving out of dependence often includes finding fault with everything the line management does as the staff manager attempts to establish a separate place by rejecting the old subservient phase of their relationship. Behaviorally, this comes out as argumentativeness, conflict, anger, defensiveness, offensiveness, and long memos finding fault with line management actions. Through all of this the power of line management is still evident in that line management is still the focus of all the staff manager reactions. The anger that has built up through years of perhaps even willing dependence now gets released. Often the pent-up feelings come out of the staff manager's anger at himself for having been dependent for so long—and so willingly.

In this stage we see the staff manager finishing with counter-dependence, often through accepting both himself and the line management role in that old relationship. This resolution allows the staff manager to begin thinking of himself as an individual, as unique in qualities and potential contribution. It includes defining an important separateness that is not dependent on being higher or lower than the line management, just different. This separateness calls forth the strengths of the individual—and the individual department. It involves clarifying the boundaries between this staff department and the others that surround it organizationally. There is inwardly directed activity as the staff department manager seeks to understand what is special about being in his position in his organization. Independence also includes standing alone and knowing what he will stand alone for. It includes deciding what he will do and will not do in relation to who he is organizationally.

Independence

In personal relationships, interdependence means choosing to be dependent on another—not because you can't stand on your own but because you would rather undertake some part of your life with the partnership of someone else. This may be a friendship, a tennis partner, a softball team, civic club leadership, or a marriage. The important common point in all these cases of true interdependence is that capable individuals are choosing to depend on each other to accomplish some important larger purpose.

Interdependence

Applying that thinking to the growth of a staff manager implies a certain maturity of both the staff manager and those she interfaces with. (Yes, we must face the reality of the line manager who is invested in being strong by keeping staff managers weak and dependent.) This two-way maturity is useful to succeeding with interdependence, but it isn't essential. The staff manager who can move to the interdependent stage will be better able to deal with the line. At the least, her perspective includes the possibility of dealing with others as equals who might share in an investment in accomplishing a larger task. That perspective alone opens a range of alternative behaviors unthinkable to the dependent staff manager.

Dynamic relationships

I am reminded of a very dynamic marriage in which two strong people have chosen to spend their lives together, working through their common issues together. It is not always peaceful because the two are so different. There are peaks and valleys, pain and progress, all accompanied by individual growth because of the relationship. Each finds the other's perspective alternately crazy or mystifying, unreasonable or principled, ignorant or enlightened. Through time the bond between the two grows, the respect grows, the trust and openness grow. Something like this can also happen at work. If you believe that ideals are important, in marriage and in work, there could be something in this analogy. It holds out the possibility that two people with quite different interests can deal with each other on an equal basis, in an interdependent way, choosing to depend on each other. We can learn something from these successful marriages, take that learning to work, and apply it to our relationships with our management, our customers, and our own professionals.

We are searching for interdependence. This is a keyword in building an effective home in your organization. Not dependence: that's where staff (appropriately) started out years ago. Not counterdependence: that's the mode too many of us are operating in today. Not independence: that is necessary in order to move to the next stage, but defines you as too separate from the organization. Interdependence is possible between strong individuals or departments who want to use each other to accomplish overlapping objectives. It must be mutually chosen if it is to work, so others you work with may need some preparation for the idea, much less the reality.

The emphasis here is on strength and desire. They are each strong enough to survive without the help of the other, and they each choose to depend on the other. Why? Because they each know that they will bring more resources to the issues at hand, they will each benefit more, they will accomplish more, and accomplish it sooner or better, than if they did it alone. That is the kind of relationship I want to see between myself and my management, my customers and my own professionals. Imagine the interactions, the quality of the working relationship, the rewards available. It is an ideal worth working for.

Picture the staff leader as a spider waiting at the center of her large web. She wove the web, giving her connections to all the important places in the organization. It is her web; she is at the center of it; she maintains it religiously. When something "hits the web," she rushes out to discover what it is, how important it is, stores it or ingests it, and then returns to the center of the web, waiting for something else important to happen.

The analogy (though a bit predatory) has some meaning for us. "The web" is as vital for a successful staff manager as it is for a spider. It provides organizational life as it feeds the staff manager with the information she needs in order to know what is going on. Each staff manager must build the web that she sits at the center of; no one else can build and maintain this web. It needs to provide access to not only information but also influence and power within the larger corporation. It therefore must intersect with the webs of other key players in the organization. "Key players" are defined by their importance to this staff manager and what she wants to do. She will build her web in a way that includes people with knowledge, technical skill, authority, power, influence, energy, and whatever else might help accomplish her larger purposes.

After weaving the web, she maintains it through regular contact with the people in it. She does not wait until she needs their help, she is out there ahead of time updating them on what is going on and offering to help them with their priorities. With this advance work, when she needs their help the relationship is already established, and she clearly is not showing up just because she wants something.

Obviously, we could all benefit from doing this. For us, the web is particularly important because of the authority we cannot call upon. Established relationships assure us of getting the information we need about important matters in the organization and also establish the privilege of being able to influence key people outside the more formal channels. With the web in place, we know where to go to gather or present information. It provides an essential, if wispy, network for influencing company directions. Without it, the staff manager is lost or at least powerless. He does not have the positional power to require consideration of others; a missing or tattered web eliminates the personal power he needs; he is left to operate within the less coordinated, less informed, smaller collection of immediate contacts required by his day-to-day work.

The web establishes your ability to talk with the people necessary for gathering information, disseminating it, and getting things done. It is a source of influence; it is not a guarantee of support. Establish it by paying sincere attention to others. Listen to what they have to say. Help them get things done. Work toward the feeling of being free to drop in on senior managers and then don't abuse the privilege.

The web starts with identifying the people with whom you need formal and informal contact. List them and get your boss's help with this list. Assess your present relationship with each of these individuals in relation to what you would like it to be. Decide on specific actions you could take to further build the relationship. Remember to keep a long-range perspective on the whole network-building process. You are doing this for what you and they might need tomorrow, not for something you wanted yesterday.

Get to know people before you want something of them. You know how it feels when someone who apparently never had time for you suddenly bursts into your office with a request for your help (especially if that request helps them and doesn't help you). Avoid that situation by cultivating relationships with people before you want something of them, fully knowing you may never want anything of them. With this positive image, it will make them more likely to meet your need when you have one. When we need to get help fast from others, we often do not have the time to establish the relationship, so we do it poorly.

Building that rapport with others is often as easy as demonstrating your interest in what they do, finding out what they want from their work, and showing that you understand. Once you have established the relationship—woven the web—maintain it through regular attention.

Working with Management

✔ **Overview**

✔ **Understanding and Respect**

✔ **Performing to Priorities**

✔ **Measuring Up**

✔ **Taking the Initiative**

✔ **Doing More with Less**

✔ **Managing Your Boss**

Overview

The top management of the company directly influence whether your job continues to exist. Include your immediate boss (we'll give him some special attention) and the people he works for. Exclude the people that your department does most of its work for, your customers. We'll give them a whole section of special thoughts later.

True, many staff departments number among their customers the top management of the company. In those cases, they deserve the combined consideration of this section and the next. Think of upper management as the people who not only pay you but established your department, approve its budget and direction, and in general have life-and-death say. Yes, that makes them pretty important.

The ideas here are short, to the point, and grouped within these six chapters: understanding and respect, priorities and performance, measurement, initiative, tough times, and your boss.

Understanding and Respect 18

"They just do not understand what the legal implications are."

"How can you deal with a management that doesn't understand basic accounting practices?"

"They won't take the time to learn the public relations perspective, but they always have time to blame us when things go wrong."

These are just a few examples of statements from staff managers struggling with a management ignorant of their function. We have thousands of ways of expressing how upper management does not understand what we are all about. And we are right (as our staff associates quickly confirm); they do not understand.

But do *we* understand? Do we understand as much about their jobs as we are expecting them to understand about ours? Do we know what goes into that "bottom line" they watch so closely? Can we interpret financial data? Or a daily production report? Can we feel, as they do, the pressures of an ever-changing job? Do we know what it is like to have to deal with all these staff departments that believe they know so much about how the line department should work?

Of course, they don't understand!

Our upper management has a clear impression of how much of this business we understand. It shows every time we talk with them. They are using that impression to guide how they deal with us, to gauge how much trust to place in us, to determine whether we really have their best interests at heart. What is their impression of us? Our function? How do we know? Have we asked them ways that allow us to use the response?

Though it is possible to get much closer to our management, most of us will never be in their position. We don't fully understand their perspective. Recognizing this can be useful in dealing with them. Instead of spending our time defending how much we understand, we can move to accepting that we do not fully understand as much as we would like to and give our energy to listening. Move out of a defensive posture ("I do, too!") to an accepting one ("I'd like to know more").

"We're trying to run a business here!"

The words may be different, but the refrain is the same: staff functions fail to appreciate that we are in business to make money, to reach some objectives, to show some results. This is not a plaything; this is not entertainment.

My response to that is, "I understand—and I'm trying to help you run that business *even* better! I am here to help, not to get in the way." You have said it, too, right? But why do they keep singing that same old song? I suspect that many of us do not understand at an emotional, gut level. We need to demonstrate what we understand rather than just saying, "I understand, I understand," like good counselors. Do we deal with the concerns our management expresses in ways that reflect an emotional investment more akin to their own? How often do we bring that kind of energy to their issues?

It's lonely at the top

A line executive has many people to talk to and few who are at her level. There are large decisions with many organizational implications. There are hundreds of people who want her time on as many different projects and priorities. This combination of forces is handled differently by each top executive, causing many to recognize that they are alone in the important things they must do.

What can we do with that information as staff managers? We can stop to consider how the world might look through this executive's eyes, how it might feel to be in this executive position at this time. We can find ways of acknowledging that. We can indicate that the work we bring to her today is not the be-all and end-all of corporate importance. We can recognize that there are worlds outside of ours and we know it.

This is not a hat-in-hand statement. It is a matter of fact. If it seems obvious (or distorted), think about the presentations to management you have observed in which the staff person presented all of the research and methodology without considering that this background was not important to what management needed.

T his about how you talk about your upper-level executives with other staff managers. Think about what you say to your spouse about your boss or your boss's boss. Think about the higher-level managers in the organization you have difficulty working with. How is your respect for management reflected in the above thoughts?

I am not suggesting that you should respect everybody you work with. My point has more to do with the consequences of feeling respect or disrespect toward a manager: whatever the feeling, the manager is going to know it. Over the long haul, it will show. You are mistaken to assume you are clever enough to hide disrespect or fake respect for any length of time. The manager in question will know something is awry.

Your respect shows

To gain respect, be respectable

Consider the upper management people from whom you want respect. In what ways do you want them to respect you? What would you have them say about you if you could put words in their mouths? (Take a minute to say the words you would like them to say.) Now, what actions could you take that would cause them to use those words about you?

Many executives look for people they can gather around them, who will work with them on their terms. You earn their respect by taking actions they consider worthy of their respect. You may find that what your management respects is different from what you would ordinarily do. But is it in conflict with what you value? If not, consider doing it and what that might gain for you. Look for creative alternatives that allow you to raise yourself in their eyes while meeting your own needs.

For example, a data processing manager labored under a vice-president who respected "completed staff work." For the manager this meant preparing long, laboriously documented project reports rather than the more casual presentation that he preferred. Repeated attempts at being casual earned him less respect for his professional abilities, and this was reflected in his performance discussions with the vice-president. The manager weighed the respect he wanted from his VP against the need to follow his more informal approach and decided to give the VP what he wanted. The result? More up-front work for the manager within a structure he did not prefer, less down-the-road challenges to his work in process, smoother performance discussions, and more respect.

Respect the past

Somehow acknowledge that there have been people with ability and ideas in this organization before you came along. In fact, it is the base they established that you are trying to build on. Without them, you would not be doing what you are doing right now. In your proposals to move the organization ahead, you are trying to learn from the past without worshipping it. You do not want to leap into the future with complete separation from what has gone before. If you do, you probably want to start a new organization.

Take the opportunity to praise what others have done to help the organization move to this point in its history. If this sounds difficult to do, I would suggest you spend some time looking at the history of the company, searching out what you would feel comfortable praising. Be especially attentive to more recent contributions made by people who are still here and likely to be important to the future of the company. After you have learned this history and have sorted out what you can sincerely praise, use the information and your feelings to reinforce people and to "talk up" what this company is all about.

Performing to Priorities

19

$\mathbf{D}$o you work for an organization whose top management doesn't give its staff groups enough guidance, or hints, or suggestions about what is important? If you do, welcome to a very large and not very exclusive club. Take a tour around the clubhouse and talk to some of the other members. You will hear comments like, "They don't know what they want us to do. One day they say . . . and the next they say . . ." Or "These people I work for must be crazy! Can't they see that the decision they made this morning flies in the face of all we have been trying to do in this department over the last two years?" You can make up a few of your own.

There is only one thing worse than not having specific direction on what is important around here—and that is *having* specific direction on what is important around here! Look at the positive side of this "problem": if management is not telling you what is important, maybe they have not formulated their position on this yet and maybe you can influence their eventual position. I would much prefer to work with a management that had not yet declared themselves on staff matters important to me than have to adapt to the firmly declared position of a management that had not heard my input.

How do you know what's important?

What are the organization's priorities this year?

As you look across the staff functions, you will likely find that money is not distributed evenly. Find out why. And find out in a way that is more objective than envious, more analytical than jealous. At this point you should be worrying less about the justice or injustice of your particular share and learning more about how others got what they got.

The lessons for you are potentially many:

1. You are moved from your rather specialized functional orientation to looking at some larger management realities. In effect you are asking yourself to take on a general management perspective. You will likely ask a lot of questions of your staff peers, finding out more about how they see their worlds.

2. You will learn about how other staff functions manage themselves in relation to the same management you must deal with. You can see what allows them to be more or less successful with your mutual bosses. You can borrow their ideas—and perhaps give them a few of your own.

3. You establish relationships with your peers that can be quite useful in future work you do together.

4. You find out more about what is going on in this organization; you are really learning about how it works and what the realities are of getting things done.

Time and priority

Money enables you to bring the resources together to get the job done; time with management enables you to build their confidence in what you are doing. If you cannot get enough of their time, watch out! The ways top management spend their organizational dollars and their management time are both indicators of their priorities.

Some of us prefer less visibility with our management—or use that as a rationalization for the way things are. A staff manager who doesn't get much management time is likely to be in charge of a low-priority function or does not have management's confidence or both. (Note: I said "likely," not "certainly.") Getting things done that are important to the organization requires the careful consideration of the people in charge. This does not mean rushing a memo by the president for her signature, or a ten-minute management committee presentation that no one comments on, or the EVP's quick approval of a new procedure manual. Rather, it means the opportunity to discuss important staff issues with the line management affected by them. It means establishing a relationship that allows you to drop by without an appointment to check out an idea with your boss's boss. It means being able to argue a point with a higher-level manager, toe-to-toe, in a way that lets you both know you have been heard.

These time-related examples imply a lot about the quality of the time you spend; quantity is not enough. Without the quality, you won't get the quantity! Time with top managers is necessary; the way you use that time is especially important.

Work holes

Newspapers know in advance how much of the paper is going to be devoted to advertising and how much will be given to the news. They call what's left after the advertising the "news hole." Parallel to that in the workplace, our top managers only have so much space that they can give to work, and they must fit into that space the most important work of the day. Often if one meeting gets crowded in, something else gets crowded out or shortened or altered. Recognizing this can help us deal with phrases like "It *is* important to me, too, but . . ."

If you hear a pattern of phrases like that from your management, you have probably been crowded out of their "work hole" by something that they think is more important. You of course know that there is not enough time to do everything that is important. Do *you* do everything that you say is important? Few of us do. Life is a matter of choosing from all that is important those few things that we have time to do. It's the same with your boss and her boss. "It's important to me, *too*, but . . ." So when you get that comment repeatedly, accept that it means your work is not important enough to do anything about. Accepting that might help you decide what you are going to do about it: is it important enough to you to do something about?

Before you launch into all the reasons you cannot get the executive attention you need, stop to figure out just what it is you want. Too often we disable ourselves by refusing to think further about what we see as impossible dreams. Our work associates give us support because they are not getting what they want, either. The result is that our energy goes into griping about management-who-won't-even-listen rather than into creatively exploring what we can do to get more of what we want.

Money and priority

Money is a primary indicator of management priority. Believe it. You don't have to like it, but believe it. If you need it and you don't have any, that's trouble because you will not be able to do what you want to do. Listen to your boss's explanations about why your budget was cut and look around to see whose wasn't. What are the management priorities right now? "We really wanted to give you more to work with . . ." "Please don't see this as meaning you aren't important to us . . ." "This really isn't the year to make our move in your area . . ." All are sincerely expressed and well-intentioned comments to help you understand that we are putting resources in somebody else's basket—or perhaps that there aren't any resources at all. Again, take a look around.

Succeed on their terms

Organizational success is usually on other people's terms—terms not necessarily inconsistent with your own, but their terms nevertheless. Showing respect for the established ways most of the time allows you the trust, the room you need, to make the important changes you want to make some of the time. The people you work with need to know that you can do well on their terms to operate confidently with you.

This is not to say you should do it all their way; that is certainly not the prescription for making things happen in an organization. Just recognize that if you have not established yourself as one who respects and understands the system, people will deal with you more cautiously and see you as an outsider—one to be defended against.

We all know the bright staff professional with wonderful ideas who doesn't get them accepted because of the way he goes about trying to change things. The more established management finds ready justification for dismissal of his good ideas in the fact that he doesn't show proper deference, or doesn't follow the rules, or doesn't speak well enough often enough of the organization. The result? Lots of useful ideas are slowed or stopped on their way to implementation. And the professional with all the bright ideas finds confirmation for his doubts about the way we do things here—and he seldom gets the constructive coaching he needs to help him learn that bright ideas truly are not enough.

Keep saying and doing the same things long enough and clearly enough in ways that they can hear, and they will begin to understand what you are saying. Do not expect new ideas to be heard and accepted the first time around. If every new idea in this organization were given the same respect you expect for yours, what would the impact be? We must acknowledge that the major share of new ideas that come along should not make it to implementation. But the organization does need some mechanism to ensure that new ideas are respected while the primary work of the organization continues.

Patience, perseverance, consistency

Predictability and performance

Many people around you want you to be fairly predictable; they trust predictability—and distrust its opposite. So they are all trying (or already have tried) to figure you out so they will know how to deal with you. Take advantage of this inclination and figure out how you want to deal with them and how you want to be perceived by them. List ways in which you would like to be viewed in this organization. How would your top management describe you—if you could have your way? How would they describe your technical role? The way you carry it out? The way you interact with them and others? How do those words fit with the way you are now presenting yourself to them? Are you putting yourself forward in ways that support the image that you say you want?

Here's an example. The management group of a department was merging with a much larger division. The department took some pride in being labelled a scrappy, resourceful, maverick type of organization as they looked at themselves. As they looked at how they wanted to be seen by the management of the organization they were becoming a part of, they used words like "cooperative," "open," "good listeners," "team players," and "unselfish." They were then faced with the inherent conflicts between how their past preferred behaviors fit with their future desired image. They had to make some choices.

I am not suggesting that you squeeze into the pigeonholes that others have built for you. I *am* recommending that you take a look at the differences in perception and behavior that contribute to how you are seen. With all that information you are in a much better position to choose behavior that gets you what you want.

Success patterns

Successful and progressive staff management involves risk. We talked more about risk earlier; it is essential for excellent staff management work. Management will limit the risk they approve until you have a success pattern, established and respected by the organization. Many good ideas for organizational change have gone by the wayside because the top management was not willing to risk implementing the idea with an unproven staff manager. Approvals of significant organizational change proposals usually go to people seen as successful in the organization already.

Success is not built through one resounding accomplishment. Every one helps, but success is really based on a pattern of accomplishment, not a flash in the pan. Building an image of yourself as an effective contributor depends on being successful through time with two, five, nine projects. Some of us must overcome an image of being less reliable, which is even harder to do. The political realities of large organizational life often provide lagging images to people in which the reputation of today is based on actions of yesterday (often as not, by your predecessor). No matter who built that old image, you will have to live with it until you have established an updated, positive performance pattern to replace it. Do not waste energy explaining how that old image really doesn't belong to you. Instead, use your energy to accomplish something today.

Measuring Up 20

**Measuring
what you do**

A staff manager with a high need to measure contribution to the bottom line is doomed to a life of frustration at the least. If you need to say "This company made $3 million more this year because of me!"—forget it. If you thrive on closing deals, making sales, getting products out the door, those needs will not be met here on a regular basis. Staff work does not bring the satisfactions that come with measuring outcomes. You want measurement? You've got 20 percent more work to do this year than last, and a 5 percent increase in budget. That is the measurement we experience most. It is like our contribution is cutting ourselves back— when looked at from this dim perspective. Taking that line of reasoning to its logical extreme is fatal to our functions.

The best measurements we can make are still a few steps removed from that measurement of all measurements: the bottom line. We are not responsible for that. We are not responsible for it and yet we have to respond to it. That's a helluva situation, isn't it? But that is the nature of staff jobs. If you doubt it, talk to me again during your company's next economic downturn. Tell me about your contribution then. If you aren't really feeling the pressure in those tough times, then top management has lost perspective on what is important.

Because of our own concerns about the value of what we do for the company, we take various stances toward others in explaining our contribution. Some of us hide, hoping not to be noticed. Others attempt to project the image they believe will sell. Others calculate; they put together numbers that they say demonstrate their impact on the bottom line. Others educate, patiently explaining their function to others who will listen. Others just work and neglect their image in the corporate community. There is something to each of these stances—and they seldom work well for us if used alone. Combinations of performing, marketing, planning, and educating are more likely to increase our effectiveness than any one approach taken alone.

Make yourself accountable

Expect to be measured by your top management. Demand it! Too many of us spend too much time avoiding evaluative contact with top management. "They wouldn't understand what I'm doing." Or "What if they don't like what they see?" Our fear that they may take drastic action (like cutting out a favorite project) can result in an overprotective posture. This distances us from what their primary concerns are while maintaining their ignorance of what our function is about. All of this can lead to just what we feared and what caused us to be protective in the first place: namely, to be cut in some drastic way because management didn't understand.

Management measures what is important to them. Are they measuring your function's contribution? Look at whom/what they keep track of in the organization and how they keep track. How does that compare to the ways they keep track of you? And, more important, how should it compare? How much should they be following what you produce, considering your impact on organizational objectives?

Although it is difficult to operate with people beyond our control and with greater organizational authority, that is exactly what we must do.

W hat are the organization-wide systems that your top management values? What do they measure systematically and regularly? What do they follow, pay attention to, read regularly, give time to, monitor, honor? Look at the relationship between these priority systems and your function. How are they connected? Or how could they be connected? How could your function become part of these systems that management follows so closely?

For example, the operational planning and budgeting system is well developed (and honored) in many organizations. You probably participate in it now, making your input about your intentions and needs for the coming year. Let's assume that you have to make your input by September 15, in accordance with the planning cycle—at the same time everyone else (including your clients) has to make their input. Now, what could you do one month before mid-September that would help your clients prepare their initial plans with your function at least partially in mind? What can a purchasing department, or a personnel department, or a public affairs department, or a legal department, or an auditing department do that will influence their line clients to think about their staff function at this early planning stage?

For example, a capital expenditures group can send their clients a complete listing of this year's expenditures in a format that aids in preparing next year's budget. A human resource planning function can track this year's people movements against projections in the strategic and operational plans, analyze the numbers, and recommend actions for the upcoming planning period. A training director can include a worksheet with the operational plan to aid managers with their training plans for the coming year.

Hook into key management systems

M ost staff managers have (or should have) occasional contact with executives senior to their immediate boss. This usually involves a prepared review of the function's accomplishments plus an overview of plans for the coming period. If you are not doing

Top management reviews

this now, think about it. What would be the value to the organization? What would be the value to your staff function? The assumption behind these meetings (one to four per year) is that there are people at least a level or two above your immediate supervisor who could benefit from knowing more about your function.

This assumption does not always fit a staff manager's situation, but if you manage a discrete staff function, it probably applies to you. For example, if you are the manager of compensation, reporting to the personnel vice-president, you manage a discrete staff function—no one else has responsibilities similar to yours. There is a good chance that executives at your boss's level and above should be hearing about compensation at least once a year.

If, on the other hand, you manage the western region of the purchasing department and are one of four regional managers, there is less need for people senior to your boss to hear from you—since you do not manage a discrete function (though your boss does). The distinction is important. Though I favor visibility for staff managers with senior levels, it is important that the time spent serve the organization well. Visibility for the sake of the staff manager's ego is not a good enough reason. Take an organizational perspective on it. Will it help the senior management do their jobs better? Will it educate them in an important part of their responsibilities? Will it give them a better sense of how their organization is performing or could perform?

Look at the potential advantages these reviews offer:

- You can educate management on what you do for the organization.

- You can market the services you provide that you believe can be best used by the organization.

- You are prepared, in charge, and have them working within your structure. It is a very fine opportunity to look good.

- You can tell them what you have accomplished since the last time you reported to them.

- You can present your priorities for the upcoming time period.

- You can get their endorsement (or alteration) of those priorities. This support can be very important when you are making future decisions about which work to do and which to put aside.

- You can show them how your work supports their mission, goals, objectives, and plans.

- You can express appreciation of their support and their people's willingness to aid your staff group.

And what are the risks? Here are a few:

- You are on display, and there is the possibility that you will not come out of this looking as great as you hoped.

- Though you are providing the structure, you are meeting on their ground, and most executives are not averse to reminding you of this if they are not getting what they want.

- Meeting with the management team two to four times a year does make these few, short events inordinately important in relation to the time they consume.

- They can ask questions that distract the whole group from the main points you are making—and get in the way of the education and marketing you are trying to do.

- You run the risk of preparing to talk with them about your performance, plans, and priorities, which may not coincide with their priorities.

Notice that the list of advantages has a lot to do with the substance of your work while the list of risks has more to do with the meeting process and how well it goes.

Taking the Initiative 21

Decide what needs to be done and do it

"Why doesn't my boss tell me what he expects of me?"

"Management just won't say what they want done!"

"If she would just tell us what she wants, we'd be glad to do it."

Familiar words? We hear them many places in the organization—especially in staff departments. Let's look at what is implied by statements like the three I have listed. Who knows best? Who is at fault? Who is the focus of this crying? What kind of a statement might we be making about them through these three statements? It might go something like this: "Top management knows everything they need to know to run this organization effectively. Their role is to tell us; our role is to do it." For some of us this describes accurately how we want to work with the management of our organization. Others of us find it way off the mark.

Another perspective on dealing with management could put us in a more active, initiating role. Instead of waiting for management direction, we could tell management where we think we ought to be going. Assume that senior management thinks it is your job to tell them what this organization ought to be doing in regard to your staff function. Maybe the reason they are not giving you the guidance you are asking for is that they don't know what to do. Maybe they don't even know guidance is important. So you are waiting for them while they wait for you. Guess who ends up the stronger and who the weaker in that little scenario.

"May I help you?" vs. "I can help you!"

Staff functions no longer need wait to be called upon; staff functions *cannot* wait to be called upon! In the "old days," when organizations were much smaller, we staff people were hired to do what the boss didn't have time to do—even though he knew how. He'd hire "staff" and tell 'em what to do and check to see how well they did it. When they "did it," they would stop and wait for what the boss wanted them to do next. He knew best. They knew it; he knew it. Those were the "old days." They are gone— or should be, in most cases.

Nowadays it's different. There is so much going on in these large organizations that the boss doesn't know about and can't know about. Instead, she hires experts who tell her what the organization ought to do. And those experts cannot wait until the boss asks whether something important is going on. No, they must anticipate the needs of the organization in their particular realm of expertise and advise the management ahead of the critical events so that management can make informed decisions. No waiting around for direction for these staff people. They are out front, scanning the corporate horizon, anticipating how their particular expertise might positively influence corporate direction. Quite a job—and quite a different one from the staff function of old.

And the rewards for being in this kind of role are obviously quite different, too. As different as night and day. As different as responding and initiating. As different as being called and stepping forward. As different as dependence and independence. There is satisfaction for many of us in doing what we are asked to do and doing it well. But the reward received is not anything like that which comes from finding a potential problem, then bringing it to upper management's attention so they can act on it before it gets out of hand. Quite different. The reward from doing your own job well and letting others take care of theirs is a lot different from the satisfaction of joining with the manager of another staff function to pursue an opportunity that involves both of you. Quite different. Or the difference between answering a series of questions about your function and presenting a recommendation to a management committee on how your work could impact their actions. Quite different again.

Many of us find reward in both the arenas that I am contrasting— at least I do. Some of us find that almost all of our present rewards are confined to the more traditional staff management side of the ledger—namely, doing what we are asked to do, doing our own job well, or answering questions others ask of us. Not bad, and there is more available—which some of us want and others do not. Because there is a price.

"You asked us to initiate; you told us to risk. What if we get it *wrong*?!" I am here to confirm your worst fears: you *will* get it "wrong." Probably quite often. And this is another reflection of our narrow staff orientation, which sounds like: "If they keep us around as staff experts, shouldn't we at least get it right?" I don't think so.

"But what if we get it wrong!!!"

Our focus on our expertise can blind us to our contribution to the organization. To exaggerate: accountants do not exist to account; buyers do not exist to buy; PR people do not exist to PR. In the larger organizational perspective, each staff professional exists to contribute, to perform in support of larger organizational goals. Try as we might, we cannot maintain that larger perspective. And that is why we are destined to get it "wrong" much of the time.

Express what you have to say knowing that most of the time you will be at least partly "wrong." You will miss the mark. What you recommend will not be exactly what management is looking for. They will like it, but . . . You know what I mean. Expect this to happen. Don't look at it as failure; look at it as management's gaining ownership. Do not go in expecting to "get it right." Go in expecting to contribute, to help management move toward decision and action.

This perspective is available to you on much of what you do. It contributes to your mental health as well as to the organization's effectiveness. We punish ourselves entirely too much for not thinking of everything that might happen in a meeting where our work is focal. A larger organizational perspective will often relieve this unnecessary stress in favor of a more relaxed, accepting approach to elaboration on our work.

"Ready . . . fire . . . aim"

This expression became the byword of many managers after reading *In Search of Excellence*. Staff managers should pay special attention to that excellent guidance because it legitimizes *not* getting it right. Applied to a staff situation, it means putting together your best analysis of what the organization is faced with; laying out the alternative actions; recommending what you believe the top management ought to do; presenting your recommendation; participating in a lively discussion in which top management supplements your ideas with their own. If their decision involves going in a direction different from what you recommended, you are still to be congratulated for doing professional work and aiding them in making a sound decision. You can feel good about the outcome. That is an example of the importance of not getting it right.

Have you ever presented something to your management when you felt both confident in your idea *and* certain that it would not be accepted as presented? What allowed you to have that positive combination of feelings? Your awareness that your recommendations are part of a larger process could allow you to feel positive. Your knowledge that the product of all your work is not the product for the organization—that thought could support your feeling good. "Hey, I don't know it all!"—even that thought could cause you to like the discussion in which your recommendation is disassembled or modified to meet larger line purposes.

There is another element to initiation. Think of the times you have heard a fellow manager discuss his boss's ineffective behavior and was unwilling to confront the boss. The boss continues on in her same old ways because she has not had the opportunity to consider the subordinate's input. As a result, the boss often makes mistakes. And too often the subordinate's reaction is to blame the boss for not changing behavior she never had the opportunity to reconsider!

How can you keep your management out of this fix? Is there a constructive way of giving the management the information it needs to make more effective decisions? Have you tried it? Or are you participating with the others in blaming management for not acting on information it does not have? Initiation is not confined to the good news.

Feedback for management

Doing More with Less

22

The blossoming of staff functions over the last fifteen years has given us a world of staff specialists. It's like a new Frederick Taylor has been at work on our staff "assembly lines." In the early days of the industrial revolution, Taylor helped simplify manufacturing jobs down to the point that it would (supposedly) be impossible to make a mistake. There was just no way to misunderstand what needed to be done because there was so little to learn.

Staff "hothouses" have also specialized workers down to a narrow range of responsibility, but with well-educated, highly paid, relatively independent professionals. We have used our considerable capabilities to learn more and more about less and less. What our specialist positions lacked in breadth we have made up for by pursuing our work in great depth, in the process convincing ourselves and others of the necessity for this expertise in this corporation. We were well-intentioned in what we did; we were not trying to fool the organization or ourselves; and our prosperous times allowed considerable support for our efforts.

Growth of the staff function

The trim trend

Now comes the recession and a crisis in productivity and a political shift toward more traditional values. A new management perspective takes hold, resulting in many staff professionals being turned out. These are not people who were fired because they were not doing a good job; most of them were doing a fine job. These are not people who are uneducated, or unmotivated, or behind in their technology. Quite the opposite. These are very capable individual contributors whose organizations no longer want their contributions. "Thank you very much, but we don't need any today." Quite a shock for the person who has spent her professional life performing within a narrow staff structure. Searching for what she did wrong is to no avail. She did nothing wrong. She just isn't needed anymore.

As organizations slim down, they go through an "onion-peeling" process that starts with the dry outside skin that gets shucked as useless. They then move in, layer by layer, removing those departments and people that are further from the core of what the organization is about. Staff people are never the last to go, and are often the first, because they are not at the core of what the organization does. So expert staff specialists end up on the street because they are not needed in light of new management priorities.

Belt-tightening actions

When times get tight, you come to new realizations about what it means to be a cost center, not a profit center. Upper management turns their eyes on you as they search for ways to save money for this corporation. There is no escaping scrutiny in these tight times. Most of us recognize that and don't even want to escape. What we do want is fair and knowledgeable consideration of what we contribute. That is hard to come by when the pressure is on. The following list is dedicated to getting you the kind of consideration you want from your management:

1. Do not wait until the pressure is on to trim your "waste line." Keep it trim all of the time. Yes, the parallel with the overweight person going on the crash diet is appropriate. That mentality does cause us to lose weight fast, but it does not keep it off. What we need in our staff departments is

a mental framework that keeps us from getting fat. We need to pay attention to what we need to do, to what size we need to be to do that, and then make certain we are that size now.

2. Use you human resources well. Some of us are heavy and solid, not fat. We bring more muscle to the job than is needed by the organization. We bring in heavyweights to do featherweight work. We need to pay attention to the skills we have on staff. Are we using our high-talent people often enough to justify having them here full time? There are alternatives. Some of us are heavy in numbers and not fat. Our people are capable; they are turning out all kinds of quality work—and management is not using it. How long can we carry the expense of highly capable people generating information or services that few others use? It is difficult to cut people from your team who do their jobs well, but sometimes the jobs are just not needed.

3. Give it back to your customers. Many of the functions we now handle were originally carried out as a part of the line operations. Other functions have come into being with the creation of staff departments. What would happen to our functions if we disappeared? Who would handle them? Or would they be handled? I am not suggesting shutting down your whole department but rather looking at individual services you now perform that might be passed back to the line or dropped.

4. Have your customers prioritize what you do for them and use the priorities to decide what you can quit doing or do differently. It is easy for us to start listening too much to each other and not enough to those people we are supposed to be helping. What kind of help do they want?

5. Find more effective ways of doing what you are already doing. If you weren't doing it this way, how would you do it? Involve the people who do the work in deciding how it might be done better. They have lots of ideas that are often not asked for.

6. Take a look at your span of control. There are no magic numbers about what span of control should be, but there are some pretty good "should nots." You should not have just one or two people reporting to you. You should not have more than a dozen reporting to you. And the same goes for the rest of your organization.

   Span of control is an area of great vulnerability for many staff functions. In our search for ways of keeping and rewarding our people, many of us have created quasi-management positions so we can promote capable people, give them more money, keep them, and allow them to keep doing what they were doing before the promotion. We give them one or two people as assistants who really don't require much management, but allow us to call the person a manager and fool the job evaluation system. If we do this successfully enough, we can even succeed in raising our own job a notch—since we have so many managers reporting to us. This in turn helps the boss's job. But how has all of this helped organizational performance?

7. Keep statistics. How many of you are there this year? And how much do you cost the organization? How do these numbers relate to how many you serve and what the organization is making? And how does all of this relate to similar functions in other organizations? And what has the trend been over the last ten years for your function internally? And in relation to your external counterparts? What does your professional association have to say about this? What kinds of ratios are you planning to maintain?

8. Figure out what it costs the organization to keep your department around in salaries, fringe benefits, equipment, floor space, heat, electricity, supplies, external services. According to a recent article, the average employee costs about three times that person's gross annual salary when you figure in all of the items listed above. Think of that in relation to your whole department. Go beyond your budget to those other expenses that are being absorbed elsewhere in the corpora-

tion. Coming up with something close to the actual figure is an eye-opener for most of us.

9. Figure out how much product your company has to sell to pay for your department. For example, suppose you worked for a fast-food hamburger chain and ran the personnel department. If the total cost to the corporation for your services was $4,000,000 last year, how many hamburgers would they have to sell to pay your way? If the after-tax profit on a $1.95 hamburger were twenty cents . . . twenty cents goes into $4,000,000 about 20,000,000 times . . . That is a helluva lot of hamburgers to have to sell just to support the personnel department!

Now it is not as if the alternative is to do nothing. If the personnel department weren't doing its work, somebody else would have to do it. And I am not trying to show that personnel is too expensive. What I am trying to demonstrate is the connection between the hamburgers the line operations produce and the dollars the personnel department costs. It is very healthy for a staff manager to become aware of what has to be done to get his paycheck to him each month. I can picture a staff group considering recommending a new program to management and asking themselves, "Is this program worth the profits from 10,000 hamburgers?"

10. Figure out how much more product your company can sell because of your services. Now this is a tough problem. Because we are cost center managers, we cannot claim direct and sole credit for the products of our corporation. At best our contribution is indirect and realized through many others. The simple answer is that it is an unsolvable problem; it cannot be figured out.

The danger that lurks in the simple, we-can't-figure-it-out response is that we quit thinking about the problem, and this would be a mistake. Just because we cannot determine how much more product the company can sell because of our services doesn't mean we should stop searching for the relationship between what we do and what the company produces. There is a relationship; it is not a direct one; it is important; and we should think about it often. We should struggle with it. We should find ways that help our own staffs and our line customers understand how what we do relates to what they do. Here are some ways of showing that relationship:

- Here's what we did for you and what it cost. And here's what you would have done and what it would have cost.

- Here's how much money we saved you by helping you move to a different system.

- Here's an idea we picked up while working with your department. What is that idea worth to you?

- If you had not had us do this, you would have gone to the outside to get the same service. We cost you $xxx, and it would have cost you $yyy on the outside.

- You used to have an expensive person doing this job, and now, through our help, you have the less expensive person doing the same job. That saves you $zzz per year.

- We found a way to help you reduce down time on equipment. Last year the equipment was down 710 hours and this year it was down 145 hours, saving the company $xyz.

Each of these examples is a staff-initiated demonstration of contributions made by staff. They did not wait until asked; they did not wait until tough times were on the company. Instead, they educated the management as they went along on the contributions staff is making.

11. Consider whether you are doing the wrong things right. How many pet projects are underway in your department? How many of your experienced professionals give significant time to projects of low corporate priority? One staff organization development consultant was making frequent trips to a remote and smaller division of the company to

develop the management team. He was doing a very good job while he learned much about team development. He was much appreciated by the manager of this small remote division. And he was misusing an important corporate resource —himself—on a low-priority project. He was doing the wrong thing right.

12. Let's conclude where we started: do not wait until the pressure is on to trim your "waste line." Waiting until it is too late eliminates options and makes drastic action necessary. This is a very sensitive area affecting staff commitment and performance. It deserves attention when management is not demanding it.

Managing Your Boss

23

Bosses are important, and we find all kinds of ways of emphasizing their importance. It comes with their formal role, the abilities they bring to the role, and the way they carry it out. Most of us have not chosen our bosses from a list of twenty that applied for the job. Instead, they come prepackaged with the job that we accepted and may get changed a time or two while we are in that job.

This often results in a "one down" relationship with our boss. This may make some hierarchical sense, but it also reduces the power we have to approach our work as we would like to approach it. An "equal to" relationship works better for us than a "one down" relationship. In line with a prevailing theme in this book, I am looking for ways of making you more equal with your boss so you are better able to exercise your functional leadership.

Defining what you want in a boss

This is worth real effort. Knowing that when you return from your organizational "hunting trips" you will be greeted by a boss who will support you, listen to you, hear your side, accept your actions, and understand your feelings is invaluable. A staff manager's work in the larger organization is consuming enough; you should not have to spend additional energies on difficulties back in your organizational home—at least that is the ideal I am aiming for. My ideal boss would have some of these qualities:

- She allows you to test ideas on her that are not ready for exposure to your customers.

- She does not require that you are always right.

- She lets you express both discouraged and encouraged thoughts.

- He brings you his perspectives on the organization to place beside your own.

- He gives you the encouragement you need to develop an idea when you were about to drop it because of other pressures on you.

- He provides protection during attack, adding his armor to your own.

- She guides your actions before they are taken so that they are more likely to be effective.

- She talks up your performance in the organization so that others know the contribution you are making.

- She cushions criticisms of your actions, putting them in some perspective both for you and for those who find fault with what you have done.

- He helps you see alternative approaches before you decide on what you will do.

• She helps you learn about how to negotiate the political curves in the organizational hierarchy so that you are more confident when you are out there on your own.

This supportive boss list is more than just a "wish list." Use it to measure your own actions, as well as your manager's. Use it to remind yourself what your boss does for you and thank her for the support she provides. Use it as a starting point for thinking about what kinds of support you get and add to it based on your direct experience with your boss. Use it as a guide for the actions you will take as a supportive boss of your employees.

I am for managing your boss through objectives. Write objectives that:

Boss management ideas

• Serve the organization well and move your function ahead through accomplishment.

• Make her look good to the people who are important to her.

• Motivate you enough that you wish to freely give energy to the objectives.

Find out for certain whether your objectives meet these three criteria by talking with her about what you intend to do. And find out what she wants from you. What could you do to make her look good? What represents success in her job to *her* and how could you help bring that about? It is not at all unusual for you and your boss to be seeking different kinds of success. But it is unusual when a boss and staff manager cannot find mutual supporting behaviors.

As you begin with a new boss or begin anew with an old one, expectations between the two parties are particularly important. In a new working relationship, many of the initial understandings between the two parties are less well defined since the people know less about each other and less about how the job should be approached. With time, softer initial expectations can be tied down to specific work objectives and plans. The process of moving from one to the other requires regular attention and renegotiation. The focus of this negotiation is the contract that exists between you and your boss. "Contract" is not intended in the legal sense but rather as a vehicle, constantly open to discussion that provides for communication, understanding, and commitment of you to the organization.

More ideas

If you are looking for better ways of managing your manager, this list is worth scanning. These ideas will cause you to think further about what you might do:

- Ask him what he wants you to do—and do it!

- Ask him how he prefers to manage you—and support that approach.

- Write your work objectives and plans and present them to her for review, expecting them to be changed. After approval, live by them, updating them with her regularly.

- Ask for a performance review. In it, give your perspective on your performance first.

- Risk as much with him as you expect him to risk with others.

- Manage your time with her. Make appointments; don't just drop in.

- Figure out what you *must* have, concentrate on getting those few things, and put all other less important matters aside.

- Behave toward him as you would have him behave toward you.

- Consider things from her perspective. Her behavior makes a lot of sense to her. Have you demonstrated that you understand this or do you act like her behavior is crazy? Do you understand how her behavior makes sense? Have you told her?

- Accept him as he is; assume he will not change. Quit spending energy on him. Find a more constructive use for your time and talents.

- Read articles and books about how to manage your boss.

- Tell him how you want to be managed and get his reactions.

- Spend some social time with her so you can learn to appreciate some other aspects of her.

- Be an outstanding performer on *his* terms.

- Talk with her other subordinates about how you all want to be managed and take these actions to her in a very supportive fashion.

I know that some of you have read this list looking for the answer to dealing with your especially difficult boss, and you didn't find it. You shook your head at each item and finished the list more convinced that your situation is impossible. It may be. And what are you doing about it? If you've done everything and it isn't working, read on.

The especially difficult boss

How much time have you spent talking about your boss or listening to others talk about theirs? Most of us seem to have a pretty good understanding of what is wrong with our bosses—just as most of our subordinates probably understand what is wrong with us. For the moment let's put aside the possibility that the problem is not the boss but ourselves. Let's temporarily accept the reality that many bosses are difficult if not impossible. And we are all looking for ideas on how to deal with them. A short list follows:

1. Figure out what he needs. Isolate the intolerable behaviors. Why is he acting that way? What does he want? Recognition? Control? Attention? Affection? To be alone? To avoid work? To punish others? To protect himself? Try to determine the reasons behind the action. Once satisfied that you are at least close, ask yourself these questions. Could I give him some of what he wants? If it's recognition he wants, could I give it to him? If it's control, could I give it to him? (Note: The question is "could I," not "will I.") There are some things a boss wants that we subordinates just cannot give (like formal authority or his boss's approval). And a serious objective look often reveals many things we could give that would support the boss's need.

2. Decide whether to give it to her. Will I give her what she wants? Am I willing to act to change the situation? Am I concerned enough, uncomfortable enough, that I will try a new behavior toward her? A "yes" response allows for the possibility of something new happening between you and your boss. A "no" means you have given up, or that the actions you could take are objectionable to you, or that you are just tired of trying—after all, *she* is the one with the problem, not you.

3. Act and see what happens. Had you figured him right? When you attempt to meet the need you identified, does it have any positive impact?

4. Find transcending goals. What does she want that I want? It is an old conflict-resolution perspective and it deserves repeating here. Find goals that transcend the difficulties the two of you are experiencing. Express those goals to yourself out loud. Write them down.

5. Talk with your boss about the goals. Not just by telling, but by asking. Find a way of getting into a conversation about those higher goals. This allows you to confirm that you have isolated those areas important to both of you.

6. Confirm with your boss that those goals are important to you, too. Articulate the goals with feeling and emphasize that these are goals the two of you share. Let her know you are behind her, that she can count on you to help her in reaching for those goals. Moving through these steps can remove any doubts she may have had about your loyalties on larger issues. This in turn makes it easier to work out difficulties that still exist between you on how to reach for those commonly agreed-upon goals.

7. Learn from the experience. People deal with difficult experiences in many ways, but those who emerge in a healthier state are usually the ones who learned something from the experience. "I'd rather not be working for her, but as long as I am I will try to learn from what I am going through." Watching your boss's actions informs your actions—that is an important way to learn to manage. All of us would prefer to learn from watching an excellent boss's positive example, but few of us have that opportunity.

8. Study the consequences. I know of few bosses who have a clear understanding of the consequences of their managerial behavior. I certainly don't and I doubt you do. We are simply too close to watch. Having a difficult boss that we have to deal with allows us to step back a few paces and watch how someone else manages and see the ripples (or waves) they cause through the organization—and we know what it is like to be one of the ripples. This gives us excellent guidance on what *not* to do if we want to be effective managers. Yes, seeing what to do would be helpful, but that does not fit the difficult situation we presently find ourselves in.

9. Quit. This is what we frequently threaten, so let's acknowledge it as a real option. Fortunately it is usually uttered as an oath or a threat and does not become a reality. We need to be careful about overusing it and also keep it as a last option when our other ideas do not work.

Serving Customers

✔ Overview

✔ Controlling Your Customers—and Alternatives

✔ Consulting to Your Customers—Ten Steps

✔ Building Success Patterns

✔ Managing Your Customers

Overview

At the heart of most staff department missions and plans is the need to serve their users, clients, patients, and customers well. If you really were an independent service business, your individual customers would be your primary, perhaps your only, consideration. Since your business is not so independent, since your market is predetermined and limited, you must balance the needs of the individual customer with the priorities of that super-customer, the corporation that hired you to do all this. In some respects you are like a district manager with reponsibility for sales of the company's products within a geographic area. You have to pay attention to both what the customers in the district want and what your boss back at corporate headquarters expects.

That additional complexity of having to pay attention to the boss back at corporate headquarters justified the preceding chapters on dealing with management. The upcoming chapters are focussed entirely on your customers. We'll consider how your customers differ—those who can choose to use you and those who must use you. We'll look at how those two relationships affect your dealings with them. I will elaborate on the consultative approach to customers, reducing rather than increasing their dependence on staff departments. That bias will show strongly in the consulting process offered in one chapter.

Before moving on, I am noticing that the word "customers" is not yet rolling easily off my tongue—and I suspect the same may be true for you. I am becoming more accustomed to it and I do like its association with words like market, bottom line, results, product, sales, and service. I want myself and you to be thinking more in these terms, and seeing my clients as customers certainly helps me.

Controlling Your Customers — and Alternatives 24

Our customers work with us for two reasons: they have to or they want to—or both. These define two ends of a spectrum. We will explore the two extremes briefly before looking at what lies in between.

Reasons customers work with us

What can you tell other departments to do? What can you expect they will do because you have the right to expect it of them? In its most basic form, functional authority has to do with the answers to these two questions. Your staff department is in charge of defined policies, procedures, rules, practices, or systems. Line management put you in charge; your authority stems from the line. Your CEO decided that he just had too much to do, or didn't know enough, or didn't want to be bothered by having to carry out your function personally and decided to have somebody else do it.

Have to

Chances are, he didn't just say, "You take care of it." Or if he did, he probably soon retracted this blanket authority. Instead he told you how much authority he was giving you, what you could handle alone, and how he wanted to be involved. In this respect, you are like everyone else in this organization. You are operating under some delegated authority that came from the top and probably has put you two or three levels from the top.

Your authority differs from a manager in sales or production. You can cross organizational lines and look into all parts of the organization that relate to your function. Your authority does not require that all these people report directly to you on a continuing basis; they just report to you on certain matters related to your function — as they do with five to ten other staff functions. This differs from the authority a production superintendent has over the operations that report to her. She has no authority over the rest of the organization. Her authority is narrow and deep; yours is wide and shallow.

The line source of staff functional authority can be forgotten by the enthusiastic staff manager who arrives long after authority and structure are established. To her it can appear this staff structure has an authority of its own. This perspective is then reflected in the way she deals with everyone in the organization and will not be to the company's long-term advantage. (Remembering where we came from is part of deciding how we deal with others.)

Given your functional staff authority, people will deal with you as a necessary part of doing their job. They don't have to like it, but they will deal. Too many of us fall back on this "truth" and rely on it for our effectiveness. We end up reinforcing our label as policemen and neglecting the importance of relationships to our effectiveness. I am sure you can think of examples from staff functions in your company. There are other options.

Want to

At the other end of the spectrum are those people who come to see you for help because they really believe that you might be helpful. They are not there because policy #1687 said they had to be; they are not there because this is the next signature they need; they are not even there because their boss sent them. They showed up because they think you might help. You will immediately notice a difference in the way they approach you — different from the last person who came in because she had to. You will notice they have a lot to say; they tell you rather openly what they think is going on; they seem willing to reveal what is going on in the organization; and they obviously think you have some expertise in your function. Physically, they are inclined to lean toward you rather than away from you. They seem more honest in the ways they present themselves. As a result you are more likely to look forward to working with them.

The challenge is to make "have to's" into "want to's." It is not that the mandatory part of the relationship is forgotten. Instead it is accepted and not the preoccupation of the customer who is dealing with you. Policy can be the basis for establishing the relationship, but it does not define how that relationship is carried out. Even in some of the more control-oriented staff functions, there is nothing in policy that says you have to be officious, authoritarian, or mean.

The challenge is to build on the "have to" in constructive ways. "Policy asks that we work together on this. Now, how can we do that in ways that benefit us, the company, and performance?" Think about this question often. No matter how much attention you give it, it probably deserves more. Emphasizing the job content to the exclusion of the relationships used to get the job done has been fatal for more than a few staff managers (and their subordinates). A staff department is effective (or not) as a result of both its expertise and its ways of dealing with others. Either one taken alone will not do the job.

Many of us carry out control roles under the authority given to us. In our administration of company policies or procedures we make daily decisions about the actions of other people. Was it within policy? Did they get the proper signature? Do they have the necessary clearance? Did their action fall within the law? Or their spending authority? This control-oriented role brings with it certain consequences. Being the department that people must go through to make any purchase in excess of $200 does not always endear them to you—no matter how much sense it may make to consolidate purchasing authority. One of the consequences of being in this group is that a lot of effort is spent on negative exceptions. Much more time is spent telling people when they did it wrong than when they did it right. (Maybe it does not have to be this way, but it often is.) When people hear that you are calling, they often think in terms of trouble. "Uh oh, what did I screw up this time?" It takes an especially understanding, diplomatic, and saintly person to make regular contact with others about negative exceptions and not be seen as "that SOB from _____" (fill in the blank).

The control function causes people to see that staff department as a barrier rather than an aid, as a policeman rather than a resource, as an evaluator rather than a helper. These consequences come with keeping people in line. What can we do about it? There are many possibilities. As you read through the list, notice how quickly you accept or reject them. Especially notice those ideas that you hadn't thought of earlier and try to hold off on judging them until you consider how they might work.

1. Give the control back to the people who are being controlled. Build a new system that moves more control to them and away from you. Involve them in the development of this system. (I asked you to withhold your judgments and started with a point that is difficult or impossible for many of you.)

2. Consider which controls *must* stay with you for the survival of the corporation and which controls you would *like* to retain for the survival of your organization. Is the difference clear?

3. In the case of those controls that you must retain, study when and how they are currently activated. Also consider how often they are activated versus the benefit received. Look for opportunities to exercise controls less frequently.

4. Consider how the controls are exercised. For example, if it means that one individual must telephone another to exercise the control, explore how this is done as well as what is communicated. Sometimes a little front-line skill-building can save a lot of misery for both the controller and the controllee.

5. Gather your group together and figure out what positive benefits you can offer the organization. Implement some of these ideas to help balance out your image and service.

6. Review your control systems annually with the people who are subject to them. Find out how you can improve them in structure or implementation. This also has the effect of causing your customers to consider the importance of your function and support what you do.

7. Invite other departments to see what you do—especially those that you work with most closely. Spring for some coffee and cookies.

8. Have your staff visit those other departments so you know more about what their needs are and where you fit into their scheme.

Controlling is obviously an important staff function and too often the nature of it encourages a closed, defensive posture and a way of thinking that make the function difficult or unpleasant to carry out. The above ideas show ways of making the controlling function more responsive to the corporation's needs.

Consultation and consequences

At the other end of the continuum from control is consultation to your customers. Imagine it as working on projects with customers when they know they need your staff department's expertise and they have chosen to work with you. That is a long way from control, isn't it? As nice as it may sound to be working with someone else on this basis, there are consequences that you may not like. For example, the customer does not have to work with you. She can choose to go away and handle the issue on her own. That is when you might long for a control system that makes her come back because she has to work with you.

Another consequence is that consulting to your customers in the organization does not necessarily tie you to the priority projects and systems of the corporation. They can ask you to do something that is not really very effective. And they don't have to involve you in what is important.

One more consequence: since the focus is on your usefulness rather than your authority, the individual skills of your staff are critical in how much and how often you are used.

The positive side of all this is that consulting to another department provides flexibility not available to the control-oriented staff department. You are dealt with much more positively because of what you have to offer to the customer. The customer controls the work and the working relationship much more directly, and that gives him comfort—though it may decrease yours.

Between these two extremes of control and consultation lie many other combinations. It is in these combined positions, part controller and part consultant, that most of us work. Recognition of the different types of duties we carry out can help us to understand why our customers respond to us as they do.

Moving from control toward consultation

As a well-intentioned staff manager, what can you do to reduce this emphasis on control? Try out some of these ideas:

1. Accept the fact that you can do very little in the organization on your own and therefore must depend on others to get things done.

2. Believe that you are most effective when you use the line organization to get the results you want—and least effective when you do it all yourself.

3. When you are looking for alternative ways of implementing a new procedure, start with the assumption that putting control in the hands of line managers will be best for the organization in the long run.

4. Question decisions that involve a combination of new procedures and additions to your staff in support of those new procedures. Search out an alternative approach that puts more responsibility with the line and gets you out of the implementing role.

5. Use opportunities to move control to the line organization—and concentrate your staff efforts on preparing the line to handle those responsibilities well.

6. Avoid taking on additional work just because "the line is

not ready to handle it yet." Get the line ready to handle it. If they can't or won't get ready, question whether it is important enough for them—or you—to do.

7. Recognize that when line managers are complaining that they cannot move ahead with their line performance because they have to wait for staff action, there is an excellent chance that something is amiss. A pattern of line waiting on staff is often an indicator of overcontrolling or ineffective staff work.

8. Remember that the line functions existed long before your staff function did. (Genesis does not read, "In the beginning, God created staff departments.") Before you appeared on the scene, many of your functions were being carried out (yes, somewhat awkwardly) by line departments. Do not deprive those line managers of skills in your functional area by building systems that make them dependent on you. Instead, help them learn skills appropriate to the staff systems you build and, of course, build systems that are dependent on the line for significant action and decisions.

9. Multiply yourself by building your skills into the line organization. Encourage them to take on any of "your" work that can be done on a routine basis. This allows you to focus on the exceptional, out-of-the-ordinary opportunities and problems that come up.

10. Remember the old Chinese proverb about teaching your neighbor to fish rather than giving him a fish. Too many staff managers are building huge fishing fleets and fish markets rather than teaching line organizations how to fish and cut bait.

These ten points all come out of the same perspective. It is one which says that your long-term effectiveness in the organization will come from building the line's abilities to deal in your function. As they understand it better, they will use it better, incorporating what they know in their management decisions. This perspective also involves considerable respect for the abilities and intentions of others. With that comes a trust that they will do what they see as being in the organization's best interests; that it's going to turn out okay, even if you aren't there to watch or guide every action—or maybe *because* you aren't there to guide every action.

The impact of the "have to" on you

Just as the customer has no choice, so it is for your department. In negatively charged situations, it is easy for us to become as resentful of customers as they are of us. The situation is often constructed like this: the staff department has functional authority over a system that all others in the organization must support—financial and human resource functions are typical examples. When everything is working well within the system, nothing is said. No credit is given to either the staff department or the customers. If asked about this, a likely response is "This is the way it is supposed to work. Why should we be praising people for doing what they are supposed to do?!" When things go wrong, all hell breaks loose. Charges and countercharges fly back and forth: "You're not filling out these forms accurately or getting them in on time!" "When we do get things in on time, you take forever to process them—plus your people don't know what they are doing."

The net result is that good performance is taken for granted and expected to be forthcoming without reward. Poor performance gets a lot of attention and results in many people feeling negatively about their work and their associates. Multiply this little scenario by the number of people in your department, extend it out into time, and you have the prescription for a very unhappy set of staff department employees and customers. Here's what you can do about it with your staff:

1. Give recognition for doing what is expected. People like to know they are appreciated for what they do. Do not confine your praise to the exceptionally high performance.

2. Set up an internal rewards system that lets people know that if they just keep the system working, that alone is good performance.

3. Find ways to keep track of how well your functional systems are working; reinforce what people are accomplishing rather than what they are not accomplishing. It's a matter of emphasizing the positive.

4. Solicit feedback from your customers on what your people are doing well. Pass this back to your people and find ways of capitalizing on it.

5. Spread good ideas throughout your department, giving credit for those who originated them. Ask people for their ideas and use the ideas you receive. Do this regularly, not just on a one-shot basis.

6. Solicit ideas for both how to do the work of the department better and also how to work with the customers better. This helps educate the staff on the importance of both being good at what they do and good at dealing with others.

7. Wander through your department and talk up what people are doing. Confine yourself to informal, positive discussions of work. Do not find fault or act on anything you see wrong if it can possibly wait until later. Do this often enough that your people begin to see your casual visits as supportive rather than critical.

8. List some important but routine tasks performed in your department that get little if any recognition. Figure out what you could sincerely praise about performing these tasks. Next decide how you could deliver this praise in a way that wouldn't seem too unnatural. (If it hasn't been happening in the past, it will seem unnatural to both you and the employees on the receiving end.) Next praise the employees who deserve it and, last of all, make this performance recognition a natural part of the way you deal with them.

Reducing negative impact on your customers

How you deal with others takes on special importance in relation to those customers who have no choice about you. What you work on is a given, so your main arena for making them a friendly customer is through "how" you work with them. Do these things to create a positive relationship:

- Let them know that they are important to you, that you are interested in their problems.

- Give their work prompt attention.

- Structure the work of your organization in a way that recognizes customer priorities, not just internal priorities.

- Check with your customers on the quality of service they receive. Include in this check questions related to how your people work with their people.

- Give regular, systematic attention to the development of your staff's skills in dealing with the customer.

- Analyze work flow and contacts with customers; isolate pattern problems related to how your department deals with customers; and act to solve those problems.

- Find ways of giving recognition to your employees who deal well with your customers.

- Make relationships with customers a part of the appraisal of your subordinate supervisors and employees.

- Offer workshops on consulting skills and interpersonal skills that help your staff learn other ways of dealing effectively with customers.

These ideas might be used by any department that has regular contact with others, but they are especially important to a department that deals primarily with customers who have no alternatives.

Let's talk anathema; it's time to talk about the work we are *not* going to do for our customers. I don't know how your staff department deals with this, but almost all of us have work that somebody somewhere in the organization expects of us and we are not doing it. We find various ways of not doing it—usually while saying it is important and we'll get to it. We don't do the work because it is not important enough, considering everything else we have to do. This differentiation—between what's important enough and what isn't—is what I've called "qualifying the customer." It is like qualifying for a personal loan.

Qualifications are in relation to what is most important to our established priorities. One of the reasons why many of us have difficulty with determining whom we will do work for and whom we won't is that we have not selected priorities. Our orientation is one that says everybody is important and we expect to do it all. In fact, if you look at the bottom of the file cabinet or in the "work pending" folder, you will find projects that we never quite get to. So we do make an unacknowledged determination of where we'll spend our efforts.

Ask me to do something for you and you may hear, "We haven't got time—we're just swamped right now." That is one excuse that everybody understands, even when they don't accept it. But it doesn't answer this question: In all your busyness, are you working on the right things? Again, the question of priorities surfaces. Let's work through a short priority-establishing list that can help you qualify your customers and decide what work to do.

Doing the "right" work

1. Revisit that section of the book that dealt with staff department vision, mission, philosophy, values, goals, strategies. The process outlined there, carried out completely, would allow you to know what your long- and short-term priorities are and how those priorities fit with where the larger line organization is going. Using that process as a backdrop, we could make this a one-step process, but there are other ideas that can help you deal with your customers.

2. Make sure that your priorities are supported by the highest levels of the line organization your staff department does

work for. Push for a twice-a-year review of what your department has done during the last six months and what it intends to do over the next six. Ask for management support of those priorities for the immmediate future and tell them that you are going to use these priorities to guide what you do—to decide which work to accept and which to reject.

3. Be very loyal to the plans you have put before management. Use them to decide what you will do. Review them regularly (probably monthly) and update them as the real world moves in and tells you your plans and priorities need adjusting. Set up a process for informing your boss—and the upper management—of the change you are making. Expect that they will be interested.

4. When old work is finished, new work is initiated, or work-in-process is being reviewed, check it all out against your approved plans and priorities.

5. Keep your customer organizations informed of what your staff department is doing. Build a short, regular (quarterly?) summary report that discusses work underway in relation to plans and priorities. This is just one more public acknowledgment of your belief in purposefully performing within the organization's needs.

6. All of the earlier points prepare you well to deal with your own staff and managers of customer departments who come to you with work your department could do. They are more likely to know what you will measure their suggested work against. Ask them to explain to you how their desires fit with the priorities.

7. Determine the boundaries of your customer system(s). Most of us work for one large organization and within it have a number of customers. We may be at corporate headquarters and be responsible for the legal work in three subsidiaries, or we may work out of a regional office with six districts we provide training for. So, at the same time, we have both one

large customer and a number of smaller ones that we service. It can be very useful to analyze how many customers we have in this large organization and what we are doing (and ought to be doing) for them.

8. Assess how your staff function is being carried out in each customer department. How does this customer's needs tie to the larger organization's priorities? How well is your function being carried out within this customer department right now? How important is it that this be changed? What needs of this customer are not now being met? What needs are presently being met but not out of priority to the larger organization? How much time, money, equipment, procedure, or system does your staff department have tied up in this organization? Where does your staff department's effort interface with other staff department efforts within this customer department? All of these questions both inform you as to what is going on and build your resolve to put your resources where they will be used most effectively.

9. Live with your priorities. This requires establishing them in ways that make them so important to you that when somebody comes along with more work, you are so tuned in to your priorities and plans that your first thoughts cause you to measure what is being proposed now against your plans.

10. Another way of sorting potential customers is to look at the resources they are willing to put into the project. Will they put time, effort, expertise, and money into the project? Have they got the needed authority to make the project important, to get the action required, or make the decisions? Be cautious about "important new work" brought to you by a line customer who just cannot shake loose any time or people or money to work on it—but, yes, it is important and she wants you to get on it right away. I doubt it.

11. Say no. Say it clearly; say it politely; even say it less politely, but say it. Do not lead your customers into believing that you are planning to act for them when you are not. They

would much rather know that you are not going to do anything about it right now so they can take other actions if they choose. Again your plans and priorities will help you with this, but many of us still find it a difficult task. That line manager who just left your office in a huff because you wouldn't give him what he wants may go back to his department and say a few unkind words about the staff services the corporation provides. He may understand why you said no—or he may not. In either case you have to be strong enough in your beliefs about what your staff function should do to resist the temptation to say yes to everything that comes along. Saying no is part of the way you define what your function is; saying yes is the other part. Both help in clarifying for others what they can expect of you. Of course you are looking for opportunities to say yes because you know that a yes means you are doing something that is important to this organization. And you will say yes to an important, high-priority project even if it means dropping other work that you are already involved in. Or (more difficult) dropping work that is a lot of fun for your staff but less important for the organization.

12. Say yes. As we have already seen, saying yes is very important to the staff manager in the organization. Some of us—perhaps because of the control orientation of our function—are known for saying no. Line people avoid coming to us because then we have the opportunity to say no, and their past experience with "staff types" says that we are more likely to stand in the way than to support their move forward. We need to look for opportunities to say yes. We should pull our noses up out of the policy and procedures manuals long enough to get a glimpse of why those manuals were written in the first place—and it certainly wasn't to provide job security for our staff. Looking at the larger purposes of the organization will cause us to realize the risk that is required, the larger decisions that must be made, the spirit that must be maintained for success to be realized. Numerous negatives run counter to the positive rhythms of the organization. For each time when I have to say no

as a staff manager, I ought to find eight or ten times when I can say yes. This keeps my contribution positive. Yeses are seen as useful; nos are not, at least not initially. As a staff manager, you want to be seen as useful. Say yes more often.

And when I say no I need to find ways of saying it that have reasons behind the no. "It's just company policy" is not one of the reasons; it only implies that I don't want to think and that the person I say it to should not think either. Expressing the whys behind a no in the terminology of the receiver of your no certainly helps. At a minimum, you want to pass on your no in a way that is understood, if not necessarily agreed to, by the receiver. Then at least she will be talking about the right things with others if she does disagree with you.

We recognize the importance of formal power in organizations, not so much because we exercise it but more because we see it being used. As I have mentioned earlier, many of us think of powers in terms of the formal authority that comes with line executive responsibility—which automatically means that we don't have it. Our responses to this power vary from respect to envy to covetousness to disgust. And too often our response blinds us to the other forms of power available to us. When we talk about what the line executive is able to do "just because" she has the power, we often reveal much about power's importance to us. We have also experienced the conflict of having to take a certain action because a powerful person required it of us, being in significant disagreement with that action, finding our less powerful position distasteful, and wishing that we had the power to do unto others what was being done unto us. One possible result is that when we have formal power, we see it and exercise it in narrow terms, in terms of formal authority, of "me" over "thee." The functional authority delegated to us provides us with opportunities to "lord

Misuse of our authority

it over" all those subject to our bit of authority. Our need to control what others do (now that we finally have the chance) can blind us to options available to us. This set of options is a continuum ranging from dependence on our customers to interdependence with our customers.

How much help do your customers need?

How much help do you want to give your customers? How much should you give them? How deeply do you need to be involved in the decisions related to your staff expertise? At what point are your customers weakened by getting too much help? What decisions *must* you be involved in to be assured that your function is being performed well for the organization? Some examples of less effective answers to the above questions:

- A personnel department, responsible for the appraisal system, requires that objectives written for the coming year (on the appraisal form) be retained in the files of the personnel department. If the manager or subordinate should need the objectives during the year, they are to borrow them from the personnel department and then return them.

- A public relations department requires that every public word by any employee be scripted and approved by the public relations department. This includes words to be said and visuals to be used. Travel advances are dependent on having this prior authorization.

- A purchasing department establishes policies and procedures that in effect punish anyone who makes any purchase without the involvement of the purchasing department—*any* purchase.

- An advertisement in the *Wall Street Journal* promotes a workshop in which consultants can learn how to make customers dependent on them.

- An auditing department requires that individuals have receipts for all expenditures made while travelling in order to be reimbursed. (This example came from a recent visit to a line executive's office where I found him taping odds and ends of wadded receipts to a page for copying. During the audit of expense accounts all of these little receipts were actually followed up on—at great expense to the organization.)

Your examples might be different from mine, but I think you get the point. I wonder how many examples like these are motivated by consideration of the good of the entire organization. I suspect it is our own frustrated staff's need to gain control which prompts policies and procedures like those described above.

But *somebody* approved these, you say. And that somebody was a line person. True. But usually we submitted the policy for approval; we initiated it out of some need we saw in the organization. Acknowledging that there is line complicity in the establishment of the policy does not reduce our staff responsibility for what we submit.

Each of the examples listed above does have some sense in it. From a rational perspective, it looks like it will work (somebody thought so). But realistically we know it won't work. We know about the staffs that get built to handle the increased volume of work. We know about the staff bottlenecks that are created as the work awaiting approval piles up. We know that these detail-oriented perspectives on large organizational life distract us from the organization's primary purposes and choke the life out of it.

The cost of giving us too much control is a diversion from the primary purposes of the organization. In the extreme, line begins serving staff. Line executives are hobbled by the procedures we lock them into. Yes, they must take responsibility for supporting these performance-hampering rules, but we must take responsibility for initiating them.

Consulting to Your Customers — Ten Steps

25

This chapter is for those of you who are intrigued by the consulting role notion and want to learn more. After a brief introduction, we will explore one ten-step approach to staff consultation. This presentation will be chronological and detailed.

You and your department have customers who depend on you to guide them on both a "want to" and a "have to" basis. However you get involved, two points are usually clear: you have expertise, and you need their support to use your expertise. This realization, when shared by the customer, is the beginning of a customer-consultant relationship.

As different as we staff departments are in terms of our functions, we are alike in our dilemma of wanting to get something done in the larger organization *and* not being in charge of the resources to do it. If all the staff managers in your organization got together and talked long enough, they would find that they have a number of struggles in common as they work with their customers, such as:

• How do we get them to give priority to our staff work?

• How do we get them to call *before* the disaster hits?

- Why do they expect we can do last-minute magic?

- Why don't they understand what this staff department really does?

- Why do our practical ideas so often seem impractical to them?

- Why aren't they willing to try something new?

These dilemmas come from staff managers and their professionals throughout the organization. You may echo or add to them.

Behind these common questions lie some common answers. And those common answers relate to a process for consulting to customers in an organization. We readily recognize that managing a staff department, be it administration or purchasing or information services, has many common elements. In fact, organizations frequently bring together managers to learn about how to manage better. This action recognizes that managers do have a lot in common even though their functions may be quite different. A parallel situation exists with staff departments that consult to the larger organization. Though their specific functions may be quite different, the process they share in dealing with customers is very much the same — or can be.

We have not put a lot of effort into teaching staff managers about how to consult with their customers across the organization — not nearly the effort we have spent in teaching them how to manage. Most of us have not even thought about learning how to consult as a legitimate area of study — though we are very aware of the problems we have when our departments don't do it very well.

A ten-step consulting process

This ten-step process traces the more important events a staff department works through on customer projects:

- Entry

- Contract

- Data collection

- Analysis

- Feedback

- Alternatives

- Decision

- Action

- Evaluation

- Exit

You might change the order, or add or subtract a step, but chances are, these ten steps describe what your people do when they consult to your customers. The process starts with the initial contact with a potential customer and ends when the work is done. The pages which follow offer explanation and guidance on each of the ten steps. Each step includes a list of thoughts seen as helpful in performing the step better. As you read through this process, think about how it relates to what your department does. Paying close attention and making notes allow you to become more aware of the consulting process you would like your people to follow as they work for you. When you know what consulting process you want to use, then you can exercise your managerial responsibility in developing your people to use that process.

You may not have thought about the process in this way because you are so much in the middle of your work, but somehow you get started. With each new project, even with an old customer, you start again—though not from scratch. Let's deal with this step as if the customer called you and asked for some help. That is the

Entry

way I will discuss it, though my comments can apply to situations in which the customer didn't call, but you showed up.

Here are some ideas I have found useful when a customer calls with some work in mind:

1. Customers usually call because they have a problem; sometimes they call because they have an opportunity. There is also a good chance that they have tried something else before calling you. It is common for staff departments to be called in as a last resort or when the problem is very hot.

2. Customers often have a specific solution in mind; that is why they decided to call you. If you are in the training department, they called because they think training is the solution to their problem. They may be right. On the other hand, . . .

3. Respect the customer's willingness to act on this problem. The fact that she called you indicates a willingness to do something about it. A good way to start things off badly is to imply that if the customer hadn't screwed things up in the first place, she wouldn't have to bother you.

4. Start where the customer wants to begin, rather than where you would prefer to begin. The customer has a story to tell and needs to tell it. The need is often more important than the story. Listen to both and demonstrate your respect for what the customer has to say and the feelings that come with that.

5. Notice the parts of the problem that seem particularly important to the customer. Listen carefully to what the customer has to say. Demonstrate that you understand through facial expressions, nonverbal behavior, and repeating back to the customer what you have heard in your own words.

6. After hearing the customer out, restate what you think you have heard in terms of what you think the customer wants. Check this statement with the customer to make sure you are accurate.

7. Establish your interest in helping the customer solve the problem. Tell the customer that you want to help, that it is interesting to you, that it sounds very important, that this is a real opportunity for your department to contribute—whatever you can sincerely say that shows the customer you want to work on this.

8. Explain what resources you have to draw upon in your department. Describe related experience that you have had. Let the customer know that he is in good hands—if that is the truth.

9. Describe how you like to work. This means you have to know this ahead of time. How closely do you work with customers? How involved will they be in what you are doing? How much freedom do you like to have?

10. Do not take over the customer's problem and make it your own. If she originally called with a problem she saw as her own, this first meeting should leave her feeling that she has a problem that she is getting help on. But it has not become *your* problem that she can now forget about.

11. Ask for copies of readily available materials that relate to the problem described. Make this very preliminary so you are not overwhelmed with data.

12. Arrange meetings with two or three others who could give you their perspectives on the situation. This will help you in deciding how to attack the problem. Short meetings will do at this stage.

13. Schedule your next meeting with the customer before you leave this one, telling the customer that the next time you get together you will propose a way of attacking the problem.

14. At this point your need to know more is likely conflicting with the customer's need for action. This will be true all through the process, and you need to find ways of meeting both needs.

15. You need to get far more information before committing to an approach because the way that the customer initially defines the problem is often not the real problem. The customer sincerely believes that the problem is as he defines it, and it may be. But often it isn't.

16. As you close this meeting, ask the customer how the meeting went. Is he getting what he expected? Asking this question legitimizes the customer talking about how this consulting process is going at this early stage. Later on, you will be talking about this a lot more.

17. If you stick with the Entry step, this first meeting will not be too long—about an hour. If it is much longer, you have probably begun to work in some of the other steps of the process.

18. Between now and the next meeting with the customer, read the materials you have collected, attend the meetings you have set up, design Data Collection, and think through Contract.

Contract

This step involves clarifying what you will do for the customer and coming to agreement on that. It is not a contract in the strict legal sense, though its outcomes are best written so you can later recall what was decided. The contract meeting deals with these types of questions:

• What is the problem? (Identify what is wanted vs. what exists.)

• How will you approach the problem? (Consider the sequence of steps.)

• How will you use to collect information?

• Who will be involved?

• How much time will it take?

- What is the customer's role? What is your role?

- When will what happen?

- How much will this cost? (Include time, money, equipment, materials, etc.)

Come to the meeting prepared to answer these questions. Have your proposed answers that you are ready to revise as you involve the customer in developing the final answers. Your answers will be revised again in later steps, as you learn more. Here are some specific suggestions for negotiating contracts:

1. Make the contract session a business-like meeting with emphasis on clarity, structure, and understanding.

2. Test your proposed approach and its likely results with the customer. Get the customer's support.

3. Tell the customer when you will meet again and what results you will bring to that meeting.

4. Follow this meeting with a memo that describes the main elements of the contract. This way you will both have a copy. Later, check to see if the memo was accurate.

5. Set up times when the two of you will reconsider how the contract is working. The contract is dynamic and can be altered through the consent of the parties involved. Unlike a legal contract, this consulting contract is expected to change, and both customer and consultant are expected to keep the contract up to date.

6. If you have not already emphasized the point, ask the customer how she will know whether the project has been successful when it is all over. Write down the response. Return to these notes in the Evaluation step.

7. One of the greatest sources of problems between staff department and line customer is lack of mutual understanding about what was to be done. Clear contracting can mitigate that potential problem.

Data collection   Somehow you have to find out what is happening. On a larger project, this means gathering information from many sources, most often people. On any project, think about the information you need and the best ways of getting it before going after it—even if it is just one interview with one person. Here are some possible approaches:

1. Design your approach to data collection before the Contract step based on the materials the customer gave to you, the type of information involved, the number of people you will be dealing with, and your own skills in gathering information. There are a handful of ways of gathering information from others that you ought to be familiar with—not just for this consultative part of your job but also as a manager. Said differently, these data collection skills will be useful to you in many parts of your work and your life. You gather information by watching, listening, asking, and reading. You can do any of these in a structured or unstructured way. You can deal with people face to face, in groups, on the telephone, or through the mail—just like you do in the rest of your life. The key is to be aware of the information you are looking for, to consciously select and use a method, and to have the skills important to the method you are using.

2. Select methods that are both easy for you to use and for the customer to understand. If the customer doesn't understand what you are doing, chances are he will not believe the data that comes out of this step.

3. Ferret out bias. One common mistake is gathering information in a way that confirms your assumptions. For example, suppose I were to ask you to tell me your three biggest problems as a staff manager, continue with this approach through all your peers, and conclude that we have big prob-

lems in staff management around here! What's wrong? My approach did isolate some management problems, but did nothing to determine their importance in relation to your overall performance. I only know what your biggest management problems are; I do not know whether those problems would be important when put in a larger perspective. The data I gathered is good, but I misused it when I saw it as confirmation of my assumptions.

4. Don't automatically assume that the problem needs the skills of your staff group for its solution. When a customer calls and asks for my help, for some reason both of us assume that she is talking with the right person. In fact, the customer has done some preliminary diagnosis in order to decide which buttons to push on her telephone. And when I get the call and deal with it as if I have the answer, I confirm that customer's early and usually hasty diagnosis. What is the alternative? In the Data Collection step, gather information in a way that allows the key people involved to speak to what is happening on the job that dissatisfies them. If you are in public relations, do not ask what PR problems they have; instead ask what is happening and what should be happening. If you are a trainer, do not ask what training programs they need; instead ask what present performance is and what they want it to be. If you are systems analyst, don't ask what is wrong with their computer systems; instead ask how present performance compares with what they would like to be getting. Get customers to talk about what they know best: performance and results. In a later step, you can help them decide what needs to be done and how your function might be involved in that. If you decide too early, you give every indication that you are an answer in search of a question.

5. Polish your interviewing skills. Data collection always includes interviewing. There is no avoiding talking to somebody along the way—even if it is just the initial contact person.

6. Collect lots of paper data (and nowadays, electronic data). Paper data is history; it has already died, but it is an important indicator of how things have been done. Paying attention to it shows that you respect the past and that you do not regard the organization as unimportant before your arrival.

7. Collect data from everyone who might be invested in the problem and the solution. This stage takes some educated guesswork because you really do not know what the problems and solutions are. But you do know that whatever happens down the road will require the support of a number of people. And you know that people are more likely to support change when they have participated in the steps leading to the change.

8. Collect data from the management group first. These are the people who asked you to come in and help. By working with them first, you let them know what will be happening with their people, allow them to critique your approach, build their trust in you, build their commitment to the project, and get their early input.

9. Tell those you involve as much as you can about what you are doing. Be as open with them as you expect them to be with you. Know that when you are less than open, this will be sensed and will affect that data you are given.

10. Do not collect secrets, or gossip, or anything else you cannot use. You are there to help organizational performance; data you cannot use is not helpful. In the extreme, people will dump loads of confidential and anonymous data on you. When allowed to do this, they in effect are giving you responsibility for their problems. You cannot solve their problems. You can only help them solve their problems if you can use what they tell you. I find it useful to tell people that what they tell me is not confidential but anonymous. They can expect to see anything they tell me in a report, but written in a way that protects their identity.

11. Make certain that the data you collect is accurate. Read back through notes you have taken. Or give the person you are talking with the opportunity to read through what you have written. Change anything that does not fit with their intent. Try to collect data in their words rather than your own.

12. Tell each person from whom you collect data when they can expect to hear back from you and what you will give to them at that time. Make sure that everyone involved hears something back—and fairly soon. Do not ask people to contribute and leave them hanging with no sense of what happened to their contribution. This damages both your project and the future projects of other staff groups.

13. Know that the work you are doing as you collect data causes rising expectations. Change started with your involvement in their organization. The expectations will vary greatly and will not be eliminated by saying nothing is going on, or don't worry, or you shouldn't worry. The concerns here are reduced if you carry out the data collection quickly and report out the results so people are not left hanging for too long.

14. Do not yield to the temptation to analyze the data while you are still collecting it. Doing so usually results in premature conclusions and affects the way you collect data from that point forward, which biases your results. Wait.

15. Know your biases and attempt to put them aside during this step. Do not fool yourself into believing that you do not have any. Give up the notion that you are an objective observer; you aren't. At this point you want to ensure that you are really seeing what is going on in this organization. Later on you will make judgments about what ought to be done, and you want to be certain those judgments are based on reality.

16. Respect the values, norms, and rules of the people you are working with. If they go to work early, go to work with them. If they dress up, dress up. Talk their language, not yours. These actions show them that you respect them.

Analysis

Now that the data is collected, you can begin trying to figure out what it means. Your particular staff function may bring a standard set of analytical tools to this step. In that case, it is a matter of fitting the data into the appropriate slots within the tools and seeing what the results are. I will leave consideration of those more defined approaches aside and move to the difficult process of analyzing what seems like reams of data when there is no prepackaged approach to doing so.

1. Find order. That is what analysis is about. How could all of this data make sense in a way that would be useful to the organization? That sense may emerge or it may have to be imposed—or it may never come about (always a lingering fear and possibility). It is easier to do this step if your information is displayed so that you can move it about easily. For example, it is a lot easier to move around 3" x 5" cards, each containing one bit of data, than it is to move around 8½" x 14" sheets, each containing from eight to eighteen bits of data. The physical juxtaposition of separate bits of data can often help you see patterns that do not reveal themselves when you cannot physically manipulate the data. Think about how you will eventually sort the data before you begin to collect it, and then you can be sure to write information down in a way that will help analysis.

2. Sort the data three or four ways, withholding your commitment to any one of them. Don't try to finish too fast. Again, pay attention to your biases. It is safer to let them loose here—if you also consider approaches that are outside what your biases would tell you to do.

3. Get lost in the data. Do not be afraid to not understand what is going on. A natural part of the analysis process is to be confused for a while when the data doesn't make sense. (If you think it is confusing for you, just think what it must be like for the people who work in the customer department.) To exaggerate slightly, if you are not confused, then maybe you just don't understand. Being clear too early can mean that you are blind to what is really happening. Then again,

maybe you really do understand. Either is possible—which should tell you to consider more alternatives than the first one to present itself.

4. If a clear sort of the data does not emerge, then force one. This will often allow other possible ways of sorting the data to present themselves. Yes, there are times when no significant patterns exist. Sometimes it means there was nothing to find. Other times it means you have to get more data.

5. Sort and analyze the data in a way that can be readily understood by the customer. If you want the customer to believe the recommendations you will eventually make, she needs to understand the analysis that lies behind that recommendation.

6. Involve the customer in this analysis whenever you can. He can help you understand what the data means. And his involvement in the analysis builds his commitment to act on its outcomes.

Feedback

This step has to do with giving the data to the customer in a way that she can understand and accept. Acceptance of the analysis depends on her belief in the data. The goal of this step is for the customer to say, "Yes, we believe that data came from our organization and accurately reflects what is going on around here." Here are some tips for facilitating this step:

1. Give the customer this data feedback right after the data has been collected and before it has been analyzed. My experience has shown this does not usually happen. Often the customer does not see the data until you are presenting your analysis of it—that is why I present this Feedback step following rather than preceding Analysis. Yet another problem is that feedback of the data occurs after the next step, Alternatives, has been prepared. Avoid this whenever possible because it means you have to come to conclusions based on data the customer has never seen and may not support.

2. Prepare the data for feedback. Sort it out in some way that will make ready sense to the customer—and in a way that does not include extensive analysis. For example, if your data collection process included a series of interview questions, list each question with the responses to the question beneath it. This is simple and understandable. It also fits with the last contact you had with the customer management when you both explained the process to them and asked the questions of them. Putting the data before them in this way also encourages them to view the data through their own eyes first, rather than through yours.

3. Feed back the data in a meeting attended by people critical to action on the data. You collected the data, so you run the meeting. Plan the meeting to include time for people to absorb the data and clarify what it means. Allow for both individual and reading time as well as group discussion time.

4. Help the customers understand that the data comes from their department. You do not need to defend the data because it is not yours. It comes from their department. After the data has been accepted, your role shifts to being a discussion leader as they move into a group interpretation of the data. Part of this role is providing your own analysis of the data and relating it to theirs. This is a point of some risk if you have already analyzed the data and they have not seen it. The risk is that your analysis may not fit with their interpretation of the data. Another risk is that they will discount your analysis because they do not believe you have all the data you need to do a decent analysis. And, as I mentioned earlier, most of the time I have not been successful in involving the customer in this feedback step before the Analysis step. Do it if you can.

5. Be prepared for negative reactions. The step is made more difficult because the data put forth often can be seen as critical of some of the people in attendance. Defensive behaviors are common. Recognize that you are working on a project where some change is an anticipated outcome. People will

support that widely until they see that they may be asked to change something that they thought was going just fine. This feedback step is their first clue. And they are getting it in a rather public setting, which could add to their defensiveness.

6. When people challenge the data as false, invalid, or distorted, ask them for the real data. Add that "real data" to what you have already collected. Or go back out into the organization and collect more data in the places where they think you should collect it. Ideally you get all the data that is related to the issue being explored.

We are now halfway through the process. Notice how it fits with what you do with your customers and with what you encourage your people to do. For many readers, the process will be quite a different way of thinking about what they do. My guess is that it will fit—or I could make it fit if we were to talk about it. Many of us are not used to talking about how we work with our internal customers in terms of a kind of generic process. For those of you who have the greatest difficulty, there are at least two possibilities. One is that the process is completely irrelevant to what you do. That is possible, and I will ask you to put that possibility aside and stick with trying to understand how the process I am explaining might fit with what you do. The second possibility is that the process is *very* relevant and quite a different way of thinking about the consulting side of your staff work—so different that it looks irrelevant or confusing. This possibility is a potentially rich one because it could hold much learning for you if it were true. From this point forward, the process is a fairly typical and rational decision-making process. Let's continue.

Alternatives

Now that we agree on the data and what it means, it is time to explore what we might possibly do about it—with the emphasis on "possibly." Too often we rush to judgment and action; this step slows us down enough to consider all of the actions we might take before we decide on one and take it. This is potentially a very creative step since it is not limited by the practical considerations of being the final decision or action.

1. Develop alternatives against a clear, shared analysis of the situation, plus a set of parameters related to the desired outcomes—look for these in your early Contract step. Decisions made, chosen from alternatives, give the deciders increased confidence in their actions because they know they are in control. They thought of many alternatives, and they could have done something else.

2. Involve the customers in developing alternatives whenever possible. This almost always works better than doing it on your own because you get the added involvement and ideas from the customer without giving up any of the ideas you have developed. The amount of customer involvement in this step depends on a number of factors: their expertise in your area, the amount of support they will be asked to contribute to the eventual decision, time pressures, and your own ability to generate alternatives.

3. If you have collected data, analyzed it, and still not met with the customer to present any of what you have learned, develop some alternative actions to take with you to this first meeting. This is not to preempt the customer's alternatives but rather to cause you to be thinking one step ahead and to be ready in case the customer should decide to move now. Having thought of alternatives ahead also allows you to ask questions and present thoughts that stimulate the customer to deal more seriously with the data before him.

4. Don't hestitate to make recommendations. Helping the customers consider all that they could do does not preclude you from stating what you think they ought to do. When you do this, show them that you understand all of the alternatives being considered, not just the one that you prefer.

5. Present a range of alternatives to your customer. This is one way of demonstrating the completeness of your work.

6. Prepare a formal presentation to the management of the customer department. Find out how this is done and what

they are likely to expect, based on others' experiences. Then do it better. Above all, keep in mind their focus on action and results. Too often we become entranced by our data collection and analysis techniques and waste precious time explaining how we did this to a customer that is much more interested in what we came up with. They need to know about both the *how* and the *what*, with an emphasis on the *what*. In preparing a formal presentation, plan what you are going to say, what you are going to show, what you are not going to say (but are prepared to talk about), and how you are going to involve them.

7. Four roles you can perform in relation to this step are:

   - Helping customers develop alternatives.

   - Developing alternatives of your own.

   - Presenting alternatives.

   - Recommending your preferred alternative.

8. The need for action often means the Alternatives step gets left out or handled hurriedly. Too often the result is a less creative and less complete solution.

Decision

The Decision point often involves people who were not present when the consulting process began. Suggest that the following people be involved in the decision-making meeting:

- People who have related expertise.

- People who have the necessary authority.

- People who are impacted by the decision.

- People who need to be committed to the decision.

- People who need to support the decision.

Being involved in the meeting does not mean that these are the people who will make the decision. They can be used as listeners, or advisors, or decision-makers, but the boss can make the decision on her own if she so desires. Make sure that they know what their role is, whatever it is.

Make sure that people know what is being decided and the potential impact on them and the organization. They will have to live with this decision from day to day, and you want it to be well supported. If they choose a decision because you "sell" it to them, their implementation of it will be hampered.

Do not move the group toward making the decision until the discussion is finished. You must have complete and shared understanding before the decision can be made. The costs, benefits, consequences, and potential problems resulting from the decision should be clearly considered and projected before the decision is made.

Finally, after the decision is made, all involved should know who is going to do what by when. Actors within the decision should be clear on their respective roles.

Action

You are not finished yet. With all the work you have done and the customer has done, he has yet to take action that moves the organization ahead. This step is especially critical in organizations that are strong on committee work and bureaucracy. It may be that the real resistance to change is not met until this step begins. Before now, we were just talking about it; now we have planned to do something about it, and that can be threatening!

1. Build on momentum established in earlier steps by encouraging immediate action. Resist the temptation to relax now that the customer has decided to act. The really important work is about to begin; help it happen. Good diagnostic preparation and planning is often lost by not following it promptly with action.

2. Participants in the process should see the dynamic relationship between what happened earlier and what is happening now. To them it should appear consistent with what they had been led to believe would happen.

3. Look for opportunities to take specific, observable, immediate action that demonstrates change. What could the management group do now?

4. Observe early actions closely since the actions are a measure of commitment to and understanding of the project.

5. Carry out your part of the action promptly with no doubt that others will do their parts. Be a good and public example of support for the changes being implemented.

6. Support and reinforce people who are trying new behaviors as a result of the changes being instituted. Even support changes that don't work that well; support the fact that they were tried.

7. Find ways to coach and counsel your customers through their new actions rather than taking over and doing it for them.

8. Hold meetings that help people review how they are doing and what could be done to build more success.

9. Anticipate potential problems and develop contingency plans for dealing with them. Make "unexpected" problems "expected."

10. Search for ways of maintaining the project's priority through time. Too often efforts toward change die out of neglect as other urgent matters divert energy from the effort to more immediate concerns.

Evaluation

There are at least two ways of evaluating the project. One is in relation to the impact of the project on the organization. Are we getting the results we expected? The other is in relation to the contract we established with the customer. Are the terms of the contract being met? Are we working as we said we would work? So we are measuring what we have accomplished and how we are accomplishing it.

1. Do not wait until this ninth step to evaluate. Build in progress reviews of the way you are working that happen three or four times during the project. For example, provide time during a review of the data you have collected to check with the customer on how you and the customer are doing. Use this opportunity to update your contract with the customer.

2. You will usually have to initiate a progress review. Customers don't seem to do this much—except when you or they are in deep trouble. You don't want to find problems that late. And there is also a very positive side to these reviews; you can all look at the successful aspects of what you have done together. This reinforces commitment to the effort and builds trust.

3. Separate from the customer; check with yourself and your staff to see that you are getting what you want out of this effort. Meetings of the consulting staff group often result in early identification of potential problems that need to be brought to the customer's attention.

4. Do not build project evaluation as a separate project. Instead, make evaluative actions a part of the Action step discussed earlier. You want the customer to see evaluation as necessary to project success rather than tacked on as an afterthought—or perhaps left out entirely. Evaluation is important as a measure of your staff contribution to the organization. Staff functions often struggle to measure their impact on the larger organization; here is an opportunity to do just that. And you can do it in a way that has the customer fully involved, which gives more credibility to the results.

5. Expect this project to be evaluated. Management evaluates what is important to them and doesn't evaluate what is unimportant. (This may not always be true, but it is a useful guide.) Push to have the project evaluated.

6. See evaluation as an educational opportunity. As the custo-

mer management reviews what has happened, their understanding of what you can contribute is increased.

7. Consider evaluation as just a repeat of the Data Collection, Analysis, and Feedback steps discussed earlier. It is different only because it follows Decisions and Action rather than precedes them.

8. Clarify what will be evaluated, when, and how. Know who will do it and how much it will cost in time and money. This ties back to your contracting step.

9. Let involved people know that their project will be evaluated—this delivers better project results. From a positive perspective, some people will see their work as valued. From a negative perspective, some people will perform well to avoid looking bad. In either case, the evaluated project gets more emphasis than the unevaluated one.

10. Know that the persons doing the evaluation affect the evaluation. And evaluations are made more or less believable according to who does them. Which would be more credible to you, my evaluation of my work or your evaluation of my work? Consider this problem when helping select who does the evaluation.

Exit

It is time to finish and get out—at least for now. This is more difficult than it might seem, especially with a very successful project. Exiting means saying, "This consulting project is finished. If there are other appropriate uses of my staff resources, I would like to talk. But this project is finished; you are on your own."

It is common for the customer and the consultant groups to build a closer relationship. As they do this, the additional knowledge and trust of each other can suggest more work they could do together. But where does this work fit with the larger priorities of the organization? Your staff may not want to face the answer if it is particularly comfortable working with this one customer.

Consulting groups also have difficulty exiting if they have built a dependent relationship into the customer. They may have set it up so the customer cannot get along without this close staff support. It requires quite a mature staff group to help a line customer in such a way that after the staff group is finished with the consulting project, the line organization is self-sufficient and no longer needs the staff group. I believe we staff managers should have this goal in mind far more often than most of us do. Too many of us derive our sense of importance from making others dependent on us and then building our staffs to do work the line should be doing.

A summary report after project completion is one good way to bring work to a close. The report both helps the customer step back from the work and helps you collect your thoughts before letting go. Remember, however, that although you have exited from the project, you are not barred from occasional informal contact with the customer to let her know that you still think about the work you did together and are interested in how it is going. This is also good for your network of contacts around the organization; it helps you keep in touch.

When you are consulting to others, get in, help, and get out. Of course it is not as simple as that, but this is a useful way of thinking about it. Maintaining too much involvement with past customers blocks work with future customers. Get in, help, get out.

Building Success Patterns

26

As you use the ten steps in the last chapter, keep the nine hints in this chapter in mind.

These hints apply primarily to those times when you are using your functional expertise without removing your managerial hat. Some of these ideas could be useful to the staff experts who work for you. They lead to success when used consistently on customer projects.

Grow through small successes

Too many of us are waiting for the "big score" in our organizations—that one project or program that justifies all the skill we can lavish upon it. In the meantime others are taking on smaller projects important to their line customers. They are demonstrating accomplishment on these projects and being considered for other activities involving more responsibility as they earn the manager's trust and respect. Line management is hungry for accomplishment and for staff managers who can accomplish things. Show them that we can do things well (and soon), and they will use us.

That last paragraph portrays a staff strategy that has worked for many staff managers. It is not the "right" strategy; it is one alternative. In it you risk being buried in trivial pursuits; you endanger your longer-range perspective; you give yourself over to other people's priorities; you possibly lose sight of your functional priorities. But it does work for many. When it is chosen as a strategy rather than fallen into out of lack of knowledge of what else might be done, it is less risky.

Risk being converted

The effective staff manager has to be at least as willing to listen to others as he expects them to listen to him. Take off your defensive battle gear and listen. Listen for the content and feeling of that line manager you have so much difficulty with. Risk understanding that manager's message; risk confusion as you try to put her thoughts up against your own; risk conversion to her viewpoint as you understand it better.

Give your customers an "out"*

Allow some room for movement. Provide alternatives for the customer to chose from. Don't structure what you present to them so tightly that they feel they don't have any choice. Provide choices so that they make more considered decisions. This builds commitment—and risks their choosing a direction you don't want to support. Recommend what you think they should do, and let them know what else they could do.

*Thanks to Forrest Belcher for this idea.

Expect less appreciation

Have you ever noticed that your line customers don't seem to be as grateful to you as you think they ought to be? Have you ever delivered a piece of work that your staff has spent weeks on and not even gotten a thank-you? Have you ever wanted to wring the neck of a customer manager who, in one simple question, reveals that he has no understanding of the complexity of your work? If that's what's troubling you, the following might be helpful.

Of course they don't appreciate what you've done! Of course they make simplistic assumptions! Of course they don't understand! That is the way the system is set up, and it is that system that gave you a job and a department to manage. Large organizations with their emphasis on specialization (and staff functions) are built to focus people on rather narrow duties and responsibilities. Like your own. Everybody is not or cannot be a general manager with the broad understanding of line and staff functions that come with that role. That happens only toward the top of larger organizations. It is a perspective that we leave behind when we step into most large companies today. Whether it has to be that way is another question and is not my present focus. Practically speaking, most large organizations assign you work that narrows your vision and efforts to a sliver of the total pie.

And to get your job done, you have to depend on other people with other slivers quite different from you own. This is especially true in high technology and highly bureaucratic organizations. The result is that you frequently find yourself in meetings with people who know as little about your work as you know about theirs. This doesn't make for much mutual appreciation. Which brings up the other side of the coin: how much appreciation do we have for what others in the organization are doing? How much do we understand their work? What would their answers be to the questions that we posed at the beginning of this section? In most cases, very much like our own, I expect.

Accept their lack of understanding

How can we expect them to understand what we have done when (often) it is that lack of ability that caused them to call in the first place? A recent telephone call illustrates this well: a human resources consultant from an aerospace company spoke with me about a meeting he had been asked to design and run. It was with a management group in one of the company's divisions, a group that recognized its meetings were yielding more frustration than results. So they called their internal consultant. He worked his tail off during the meeting keeping them focussed on the agenda, ensuring wide participation, clarifying decisions, checking out responsibility for action, etc. The meeting went very well; they got the results they wanted; they congratulated themselves; they gave their exhausted consultant some polite thank-yous; and they left. The consultant was disappointed and angry. He called me to unload. After all the work he did before and during the meeting! What an ungrateful bunch!! They had no understanding whatsoever of what he had done!

Their behavior does make some ironic sense. The management group called because their meetings were not working. Put another way, they didn't know how to make a good meeting. If they didn't know how to make one, it is just possible they might not know the ingredients of a good meeting as they are being combined by an expert meeting-maker. It is possible they didn't know what to appreciate. They liked the results of his work and did not recognize the subtle ways he helped them get those results.

Broaden this story to staff groups in general—and your group in particular. Much of the understanding, gratitude, and appreciation we are expecting is unreasonable, considering our customers' present knowledge of our function. This does not take customers entirely off the hook. There is still a lot they can appreciate, especially related to the results we deliver, the large effort we put in, our willingness to assist them, etc. But it is probably time to let go of that need for them to wax eloquent on the subtleties of our professional contribution. It is a nice dream but better realized with our coworkers than with the people we serve, who know less about our fine work.

People are experts on their work. Nobody knows your job better than you do—and the same is true of your customers. Ask them how it is going. Ask them what is getting in the way of their doing the kind of job they would like to do. Ask what helps them do their jobs. Do not ask what financial, personnel, computer, or other services they need—at least not right away. Instead focus on what they know. Use the information you collect from them to decide which of your services they need.

Talk with people about what they know

Too often we ask line management what they want done and when they want us to do it. To the extent that we limit ourselves to those questions, we are giving away our expertise. It's like saying, "Ms. Manager, what do you want me to do. You know best. Just tell me and I'll do it." Given that there are times when this is true, I want to shift your focus to the times when you have said that and gotten a long sermon from management that was in effect telling you how to run your function. You may recall your internal reaction as you listened to the manager answer your question: "Who the hell does she think she is, telling me . . . "

Don't give your expertise away

"**L**et's not reinvent the wheel," you hear, followed by mumbles of agreement. Baloney! That expression sands the wheels of progress at least as often as it oils them. We should stop nodding our heads in automatic agreement each time someone comes out with that expression.

First of all, wheels are being reinvented constantly. I am not arguing that everybody is doing it or that we should keep it up. I am

Reinvent the wheel

arguing that (in spite of that trite expression) for some reason we keep reinventing wheels, and I think it's because we know it makes sense. Most of what we do in our lives has been done before by somebody else. Our parents were very good at reminding us of this, and we are almost as good at reminding our own children.

In corporations, this is equally true. Those who do not learn from corporate history are doomed to repeat it. And we are "doomed"; we repeat it constantly. Why? Because though it has been done before, *we* have never done it before. And we want to, need to, do it ourselves in order to believe it, to commit to it, to take pride in it. We want to do it ourselves so we know what it is like at a personal level.

Why do we reinvent a capital assets system that is available from our accounting firm? Why do we build an orientation program for this division instead of using the one that headquarters provides? Why do we design a management training program focussed on planning, organizing, directing, and controlling when there are at least fifteen on the market that we could have today and with much less effort? Why? Because we want to do it ourselves, we want to own it, we want to be committed to it, we want to believe in it, we want to be proud of it, we want to say "We did this!"

Now let's shift our focus to our customers. Imagine that you are about to install some system, process, or procedure in one line division of your organization. And it is a system that you are very familiar with and successful with and have installed twenty-seven times before. It is terrific, and the customer division is going to love it—once you get it going. But do they believe this? Do they trust you? Do they accept all your successful past experience? No.

So what do you do? If you are smart, you reinvent the wheel. Because you know that the product, the system, is not all you are working with here. You know you need the support of real people, with real energy that they can use for or against your new system. So you and your staff spend hours helping this line division look at its needs. You involve everybody who is involved in the new system. You pay attention to their needs for special tailoring to their unique situation. And this isn't whitewash; you really do pay attention. You work toward the day when they will say, "This is our system. We helped build it. This staff department listened to our needs and helped us come up with a system to meet those needs. Now that we have it, we are looking forward to using it." That is the kind of support your system needs over the long term, when you are gone and it needs to maintain itself. You get that kind of support by reinventing the wheel. It requires a clarity about your purpose and an openness to your line customers that many of us find difficult to achieve.

Do for yourselves whatever it is that you would have others do for themselves. Put another way, if you are responsible for the performance appraisal system in the corporation, use it particularly well on yourself. If you are in charge of purchasing, follow your own process when you buy. If you are responsible for legal, follow the "laws" of the organization. Do not be the cobbler's children, suffering in your own and others' eyes through neglect of your own needs. Take advantage of the fact that the systems you maintain apply to you as well as to others. Learn from your own experience with your systems. You and your staff can use this practical knowledge with the others you serve who fall under the same systems.

Don't be the cobbler's children*

***

*I am indebted to Jack Tharpe for reinforcing these thoughts.

Managing Your Customers

27

The combined expertise, authority, commitment to your function, contacts with management, and years in the organization make your staff manager role with the customers a potentially complex one. It is not as simple as a staff person working for you who is seen primarily in terms of expertise.

Your customers cannot ignore the fact that you have both expertise in your function and the authority to do something about their situation. They try to capitalize on this—as would you, put in their shoes. Your customer's focus is often narrower than yours. Customers want resolution of the immediate issue; you are trying to look at that issue in terms of the longer-range implications of alternative solutions. And if you should try to explain this to them, it will likely be heard as so much corporate staff mumbo-jumbo. (Watch for the eyes rolling up in the head—that is usually an early clue.) Add to this your present personal orientation, which usually has a significant effect on how you see the problem before you. For example, this may be the twenty-third problem you have had to face this week and your spouse and kids haven't seen you before 8:00 p.m. this month, and the president of the company is on your case about . . . well, you get the picture.

Four perspectives on dealing with customers

Dealing with customers as a staff manager involves at least four perspectives: your authority, your expertise, your leadership, and yourself. And you are bringing this complex of perspectives to a customer who is preoccupied with getting it fixed today. A word about each of those perspectives.

1. *Your authority*. This is the primary reason people come to you for assistance. You can do more about it than your subordinates can, so they come to you. When you combine authority with considerable years of experience, you get a line at your office door. Every inquiry must be dealt with; most of them are referred back to your staff. You need to establish yourself with your customers as someone who will keep a close eye on the work of your staff professionals. You will be there at critical points, but you will not do all of the work. When you do the work, you are no longer managing.

2. *Your expertise*. You have the expertise and everyone knows it. The danger is that you will use it with customers in ways that undermine the expert power that your subordinates need to establish with those customers. As I have emphasized elsewhere, expert power is a staff consultant's primary way of offsetting the authority power of the line manager. When you use expert power on a project your subordinates are supposedly heading, you weaken them in the eyes of their customer. It is especially difficult for an inexperienced staff manager to stay out of the expert role because it was expertise that allowed her to move into this management position, and she doesn't have enough experience as a manager to stay confidently in the manager's role.

3. *Your leadership*. The leadership perspective is probably the most complicated one from the customer's viewpoint. As a function leader you are concerned about its directions and how this individual project relates to those directions. Your customer's immediate-solution orientation will conflict with your future-implications orientation. A mistake we staff make at this point is to try to quickly educate the customer

about where our function is going. We often succeed in convincing the customer that his concerns are not that important to us and that we work in a different world, likely a different galaxy. Educating customers about staff directions is difficult under the best of circumstances and practically impossible when their immediate needs are pressing.

This leadership role also includes representing your function to the whole organization and speaking for it to the top management of the organization. All of the political considerations fall into the leadership realm, what will sell right now, with whom you have good connections, how to take an idea upstairs, and where your staff function stands among the many priorities of upper management. As important as all of this is to the effectiveness of the company, it often does not stand you in good stead with this customer focussed on this problem at this moment.

4. *Yourself*. Behind all of these organizational perspectives is a person who is heavily impacted by *all* that surrounds her, on the job and off. You cannot ignore the outside joys and sorrows of your life. The customer may not be aware, but you know what that outside perspective does to your dealings with customers. This perspective has a lot to do with how we act out the other three.

Awareness of the many selves we bring to our work helps us understand why we react as we do. The four perspectives can aid us in sorting out where we stand and why we might have mixed feelings. With this added knowledge, we can better explain our position to our customers.

P art of your managerial role involves deciding when to get involved in your people's work. Staff people—especially experienced staff people—are noted for preferring to do the work themselves, so this can be a touchy point.

When to participate in your staff's work with customers

Consider participating when:

- The project involving them has corporate-wide implications.

- The project will require approvals at levels above your boss.

- The project is experimental and represents potential breakthroughs for your function.

- The project is of high risk and potentially costly if it doesn't work.

- The customer is reluctant to engage in work that the corporation is saying must be done.

- The customer is at an executive level and is having difficulty accepting working with your much less senior subordinates.

- Your intuition tells you to.

- The customer is concerned about your staff's performance.

- Your staff deserves more recognition than they are getting for their work.

- Your staff says they need your presence at critical points in working with a customer.

Do participate when:

- Your staff is inexperienced, and you are confident they cannot take the next step alone.

- Your staff is in a panic and predicting disaster.

- Your staff is being threatened with physical assault by a customer. (Intervene carefully.)

- Your staff is obviously on the wrong track and about to waste an unacceptable amount of resources travelling down that track.

- Your staff needs last-minute help because there are just not enough of them to complete the job on time.

- Your planning and review process has not told you enough about what is going on. (Notice the assumption of a planning and review process that systematically updates you.)

Do not participate when:

- You don't have anything else to do, so this might be a good time to help on the project Joe and Evelyn are working on.

- You feel that you are losing your expertise through lack of contact with real customers and real work.

- You don't know how to manage, but you *do* know how to be an individual contributor.

- You are lonely.

- You feel that you have a bunch of good ideas that your people could really use on this project.

- You just can't wait for the project review that they are planning on giving you later this week.

- You have worked on this kind of project a hundred times before, and you could really speed it up by telling your people what to do.

- You know that the customer really wants you to work on this project. He said wonderful things to you about your abilities.

- You want to show everyone how important you are.

- You would rather work on this project than do your strategic planning, or a performance review, or some other management task.

Assessing your department's impact

Staff functions suffer from not finding out how we are doing until we would almost rather not know. We can be sure that our line customers will come to us when disaster strikes, but then it is often too late to do the work needed to put things right. In fact, it was too late two weeks ago. But we have no choice as to whether we will work on it—the problem must be dealt with.

How do we set it up so that as department managers we get fair warning about problems before they descend on us? We can do a lot with our own staff, and that is where we should do our first work. The other important place to be working is with our customers. They are often closer to the action and results of our services than we are, so they are in a better position to sound the first warning. Getting them to do that is something else again, and this is where your unique role as manager comes into play.

Don't expect early warnings from customers with whom you do not have an established relationship. Being able to count on a customer to speak up before a problem has reached disasterous potential is just asking too much of a person who is busy watching over many priorities and projects. It involves too much risk and possible confrontation with you. They hate to call if it might go away. So they will often wait until the problem is undeniably large and undeniably *yours*. Then they will call—and that's too late for you.

This last paragraph gives your customers less credit than they deserve. Despite its unfairness, it happens often enough that you need to be prepared. You need better feedback mechanisms, not irate customers. If you find yourself surprised too often by negative results in your customer departments, you are overlooking a responsibility. That responsibility has to do with ensuring that your staff is performing. The managerial actions you take are quite different from what you might do as an individual contributor. Here is a short list of possible staff manager actions:

1. Establish relationships with client managers (earlier we talked about weaving a web). Intentionally build on both the formal and informal aspects of your work with them, giving emphasis to the informal. The formal part of your work will likely bring you together occasionally anyhow.

Stop by their offices. Check on their problems in their work and see how you can help. Do favors for them. Show them that you are thinking about them. The importance of maintaining this network of customer managers is hard to exaggerate.

2. Ask for feedback on the work your department is doing. Do this within the context of the established relationship if you want it to be especially helpful. When you hear good things, pass them on to your staff. When you hear bad things, act on them immediately and show the line manager that you paid attention and took action. ("Taking action" does not mean that you accept without question what the line manager told you. It does mean following up in obvious ways.)

3. Make opportunities to tell them about the good work your people are doing for them. There are at least two purposes here. One is to assure customers that you really are going to some lengths to serve their departments well. Another is to educate the line manager in what your particular staff function is all about, making it more likely that whatever he says about it will come from a more informed viewpoint. A third reason has to do with maintaining the line manager's —and your own—perspective. You want him to know that you do a lot of good stuff for him so that the bad stuff doesn't look as bad in the larger perspective. The supportive nature of staff work means that it is often taken for granted when done well. To move it into the realm of being worthy of credit requires action on your part.

4. Build customer appreciation of what your department does. This is closely related to the last point and deserves separate billing. Your goal in reminding them of your successes is more than eliciting a "Thankyouyoudidagreatjob!" That's not bad, but much more is possible. For example, think how it feels when a customer manager says to you, "I am just beginning to realize how complicated your work is. I'm afraid I've been guilty of seeing it as much simpler to perform than it really is. I haven't been giving you or your people enough

credit for the importance of your contribution to our organization's success. I don't know how we could get along without you. Thank you!" (If you are looking for a peak work experience, this is probably it!)

Let's look at all that short but overwhelming statement contains: understanding, importance, appreciation, contribution, and gratitude. Understanding of what you do; knowing the importance of your work; appreciation of the abilities required to do your work; knowing the contribution you make to the larger organization; and being grateful for what you have done. That is a lot more than an occasional pat on the back at the end of a meeting.

5. Go after it! Do not wait for all that appreciation, understanding, and gratitude to happen. Make it your goal to make it happen. Sound staff performance is not enough to get it for you. You will spend many a lonely hour by the telephone and the in-basket if you expect the appreciation I just quoted to appear regularly and spontaneously. It won't, so set it up. Some of you who are more uncomfortable with the idea of seeking recognition are probably squirming a bit right now. It would be easy to mistake my recommendation for a public relations or image-building effort. And that is all it will be if it is not based on substantive performance from your department. "Going after it" presumes you *deserve* it.

6. Establish the importance of clients expressing their concerns. A "concern" is much different from a "problem," and a problem is quite different from a "disaster." As manager, you want your department to know about concerns before they grow into problems, and you are one of the many listening posts that the department can have to keep in touch with what is going on. Your listening is different from your people's in that you are better able to talk with your managerial peers than are they. Take advantage of this. Know that your customers will hesitate to bring their concerns to you for fear of the repercussions that might be felt back in your group. This hesitation should be outweighed by the opportunity present in knowing about a customer concern before it

becomes a problem. Cultivate relationships that increase the likelihood you will find out what is going on while there is still time to act on it.

7. Establish systematic appraisal. We honor (or at least give lip service to) the idea of regularly reviewing individual employee performance. Why not do the same thing for your staff department? Find out from your customers how well you are meeting their needs. Put their assessment of your departmental performance up against you own. Find out from your staff how well they think the department is doing and see how that fits with your views. This is not a substitute for the informal contacts discussed above; it's in addition to them. You may want to ask for some help in doing this from other staff departments more skilled in questionnaire and survey work than your own (like the human resources department), or you may need the help of a neutral third party—like an external consultant. If you perform this departmental appraisal regularly, you can trace the patterns over years, noting your progress.

   May most of your client contacts be positive ones. If you establish the customer network and routinely maintain it, you will end up having many positive encounters with your customers. When they see you coming, their faces are more likely to brighten than darken at the prospect. We all have people whose arrival provokes thoughts of "Here comes trouble . . . What's wrong now?" To avoid being one of those people, pursue the steps discussed here.

Supervising Staff Professionals

✔ **Overview**

✔ **Defining Your Role**

✔ **Developing Your Staff**

Overview

This section explores thoughts, ideas, and actions related to managing functional specialists in a staff department. It assumes you are ultimately responsible for the work your people do and for the directions the department moves in.

The section further assumes that you know a lot about how to manage and lead a staff group. If I asked you how to select people, how to develop them, how to talk with them about their performance plans, you would have answers to my questions. Not all the answers, but some. You have been in the job long enough, have watched others even longer, and this experience has given you many ideas about how to deal with people.

This section intends to add to that experience. You know what you get from talking about your staff with other staff managers at a conference. You get together over dinner or at breaks and talk about what *really* happens in your job. You find that others with similar responsibilities experience similar joys and frustrations in managing people. You are reminded that you are not alone; you leave with a few good ideas and a phone number to dial if you need help or sympathy. I hope this section provides a similar service for you.

Defining Your Role

28

A common managerial difficulty is defining our unique contribution to the organization. We can be defensive or threatened when we cannot see what we contribute. Have you been in the middle of a meeting with your staff and asked yourself, "What am I doing here? Am I needed?" And were those questions accompanied by a bit of panic in the stomach? That is what I mean by "threatened." It can lead to inappropriate actions like taking control, or calling attention to oneself, or finding fault with others, or just talking too much.

The risk is that you are not really needed and they are able to do everything without you. What if the people working for you are smarter than you technically? What does that leave you with? Have you noticed that your boss would rather talk with your subordinates about this project than you? And how they would rather talk with your boss? Where does that leave you? There's that little panicky feeling again.

A way out of this is defining your role and your unique contribution. What do you bring to the organization because of your unique combination of assigned responsibilities and individual abilities? Answering that question has been the resolution of my discomfort more than once.

The risks: what difference do I make

I had been a manager for about two years when the company was reorganized into a more centralized structure. One of the results was that responsibilities that had been in another division were moved under my corporate umbrella, along with their manager. He was an especially able professional and I immediately perceived him as a threat. I imagined him coming in and informally taking over my department. I imagined that his professional competence would so outshine my own that my people would wish they no longer worked for me and instead worked for him. His style, his way of thinking, and many other things about him were obviously a lot different from mine—and I judged this to my disadvantage in my more negative and fearful moments. I began asking myself, "Why am I needed around here?"

All of these feelings were good reason for me to build distance between myself and this man. But thanks to the guidance of my boss, that is exactly what I did *not* do. Instead, I acted counter to what my intuition and insecurity told me to do. I moved toward him. I found out more about him and told him about me. We explored the dynamics of the situation we found ourselves in. We together asked ourselves this question: what is our unique combination of assigned responsibilities and individual abilities? The result was that he became a consultant to me and aided me with his perspective as I managed the department. I talked with him about departmental directions, opportunities, and problems before I had formulated what I wanted to do. I allowed and (later) encouraged his influence. I did a better job of managing, and the department was more effective, because I worked with him.

Losing purpose or meaning is the greatest risk I see. . . . It is hard to imagine one greater. The same risk is felt at other major turning points in life. It is usually countered by learning new skills and relationships, by setting sights on new goals. The risks you take in staff management have rewarded others in the past—and could reward you.

The rewards of management are so different from those of being an individual contributor. For some, they are so different that they are not rewards at all—or we can never find them. They lack immediacy. We have to look in different places and wait longer to get them. They are easy for a new manager to miss. Just think about completing a project alone as contrasted with helping a newer subordinate do the same project. What is the reward of each, and when does it appear?

Their differentness and delayed aspects cause many of us to temporarily step back into our old role. Remember the weekend when you put aside the management "stuff" you knew you should be doing to spend a few hours on a project that you should have delegated? Or remember the last time your boss was pestering you for some management reports (probably appraisals) that were late because you had made them a lower priority than some technical work that nobody knew how to do as well as you? These retreats back into the old role are common and understandable. They are increased by the fact that many of us are responsibile for both doing and managing the work. Better managers find satisfaction in contributing through others. If you are getting your primary rewards through your direct technical contribution, then you are probably not managing very much. Being proud of how others completed a project is quite different from being satisfied with how you did it.

Satisfaction through others' work is possible. For some of us it is even more satisfying than if we had done it ourselves. Getting that satisfaction takes longer and often is not accompanied by much credit from others—both unique aspects of the managerial reward experience. Your goals as a manager have to be particularly clear and combined with an important internal motivation that allows you to be satisfied even when nobody else notices.

The above is true for all managers and is doubled in impact for many staff managers because we are already one or two steps away from the action that gets honored. When was the last time a staff department got primary recognition for its contribution to moving your company ahead?. The likelihood of being recognized for managing is even less. This is not a complaint. This is reality.

As a staff professional, you were satisfied through your individual contribution to the department. Now as staff manager your satisfaction will be related to the department's contribution to the larger organization. Your part in making that happen is often as hard to sort out as it is important.

Before, you developed yourself; now you develop others and get your rewards from that. It is not that your self-development gets neglected or becomes unfulfilling; there can continue to be self-satisfaction in that. A new reward now available to you is in bringing others along. Another reward relates to the exercise of power and authority. Since you now have more resources at your "command," there is the possibility of having wider or deeper impact. This increased power often includes primary responsibility for a specific staff function. You *are* "Mr. Personnel," or "Ms. Accounts Payable," or "Mrs. Legal" for the organization. That brings with it recognition, a kind of staff status, that can be rewarding. You have access to the whole organization. This is an important reward that comes with your job. It is not for performance so much as it is for possession of a unique staff function that is needed across the whole organization—and this can be rewarding.

Above all, manage

Figure out what it means to be a manager of a staff department. Get help from the people who work around you. Find out what their expectations are. Listen to what they have to say and then propose a way of managing that seems feasible to you, effective for your company and department, and relevant to the needs of the people you work with. Decide what you will do as a manager and how much time you will spend managing. Most of us have to (and want to?) do other things besides manage a department. There are the projects you work on as an expert advisor. There are the technical reports you contribute to. All of those duties are more in your old individual contributor mode than in a managerial mode. Do not deny the existence of this work; make time for it; and decide how much of your time is going to be invested in running the department and how much will be spent as a worker in the department.

Delegate

Watch out for the ready rationalizations that result in holding on to work that ought to be moved to your staff. There are numerous excuses for continuing to do the work, like "My staff really doesn't have the time." Or "I'm the only one who knows how." Or "They just aren't ready to take it on." These are quite handy reinforcements for maintaining you in the role of a working professional. In the meantime, where is the department going? Who is educating upper management on your direction? Who is building and maintaining networks with other line and staff executives? Who is measuring departmental performance against plan? Who is attending to the motivation and development of the staff professionals? When you are not delegating, you are not managing resources beyond yourself. You are not multiplying yourself. You are not leading a department. Instead you are trying to push the department from the middle of the pack. It can be done, but takes so much work. Different skills applied through others can result in a department operating in concert with your leadership.

Thinking out loud

When you were a lone, individual contributor there was much you could decide, figure out, or ponder privately. Others were often less interested in how you came to your conclusions than what you came up with. As a manager, you have to go public with your internal workings. So much of what you decide impacts others. They want to know how you got there. They want assurance that you have heard them. They want to know why. This calls upon you to frequently exercise skills that you only occasionally used as a working professional.

The skills have to do with knowing what you think and feel and articulating it to others—while you are still in the middle of working it out for yourself. This implies self-awareness and confidence of a nature that you possibly didn't draw on before becoming a boss.

Doing something different

Your department can stagnate if it moves into a maintenance stage and becomes complacent about the way it does its work. The people in your unit can dig ruts into their jobs that, in the long run, are hard to climb out of. If you have staff responsibilities that have not changed for a long time, it might be time to look at doing something different for the sake of life and flexibility. Consider new approaches to your work. Ask yourself and others how it could be done better, or faster, or cheaper, or differently. Move individuals around for their own development; prepare people for vacation backups or future replacements. Give away part of your job through delegation. Set up a task force of nonsupervisory employees to identify and tackle a new opportunity.

Each of these ideas looks unneccessary in the short term and invigorates your department for the long term. When you try one of these invigorating ideas, do not expect your work group to be overjoyed. Just when they have it down to an effective routine, you seem to be tearing things up again. Consider their perspective; involve them in what you want to do and why you want to do it. Help them understand that this is going to continue to be a department which looks for better ways of doing its work. They can expect that it will always be that way and should incorporate that orientation in the way they approach their work—a hard point to sell.

Considering what can happen without this invigoration reminds me of several cases. I recall an accounts payable section that did its work quite well without the help of and in complete ignorance of the computer. . . you know the rest of that story. I think of a corporate personnel function that was cut back severely as the company decentralized. Personnel was doing its day-to-day job well and was surprised by questions for which it lacked answers when top management decided to reorganize. I think of a traffic manager of six years who had to be replaced from the outside because she had not groomed a replacement. These situations lent themselves to some advanced thinking and movement in the department so as to better meet the future.

O ne of your roles as staff manager is to make sure your people have the time, energy, and resources to do the work of the department. To do this, you will have to protect them from organizational intrusions like paper, politics, and people from other departments. One of the better ways of doing this is having performance objectives so compelling that your people will protect themselves by putting aside those lower-priority intrusions in favor of their real work.

Protect your staff

T he organization learns what your department is about through your staff professionals. And image is important! Do not deal with it in isolation from performance. That kind of hype is usually recognized. Build your department's image through building your staff's performance. Help your professionals recognize that they are representing the department and that it is important to all of you that the department be seen in a way that fits with the contribution it is making. This can mean emphasizing how you helped a customer so he has a greater appreciation for your importance to the company. It can mean asking someone to put in a good word on your behalf. Or it can mean a management presentation with the primary purpose of visibility. All of these actions are legitimate when building from a base of solid contribution to the company.

Image conscious

Y ou are a model of leadership, of management, of consultation, of technical expertise, of an individual. People working for you look at how you carry out each aspect of your job and

The model manager

observe how your behavior supports what you say you are trying to accomplish. You do not have to ask them to do this; they are doing it now. Chances are, they spend far more time thinking about your individual performance than you spend on theirs. The difference is that the company requires you to talk with them about how they are doing. But many of them don't talk to you about your performance. They think about it and may discuss it with others. Encourage them to tell you what they think. Do this in a way that allows you to listen and allows them to be open.

The larger point is, like it or not, you are a model. And your modeling is a powerful way to influence the people who work for you. Since you are influencing them already, why not find out more from them about how you are influencing them. See how their words fit with what you are doing. Then make any changes you want to make and see how your new approach works. Where is it written that a boss can't learn? Being open with your learning encourages them to do the same.

Developing Your Staff

29

There are three primary elements to building a staff: finding them, developing them, and keeping them. I'm going to write about the first two. If you do these well, the third part often follows. My emphasis throughout this chapter will be on individual growth. Occasionally it will sound like I am shortchanging the organization in favor of the person. Most of this book emphasizes organizational results, so I think it is appropriate to concentrate a few pages on your staff professions' growth.

Consult the business shelf at your bookstore for more generic information about growing employees of all kinds. Look upon the following pages as a specialized supplement to that other valuable reading.

This is a most critical step, and it should be done thoughtfully. Here are a few points particularly important to a staff manager:

Selecting staff

1. Select diversity of perspectives, technical backgrounds, and personalities. Hire people you can learn from and vice-versa. Build a team that represents a range of views, ages, sexes, races, and that shares a bond of professional competence.

2. If you need a particular brand of expertise now, it is faster to hire it than to grow it. Go get it and do a good job now rather than grow it and struggle with performance for two years. Although it is important to grow people into new responsibilities, you cannot anticipate every need the company might have. You may need a particular kind of expert tomorrow and not be able to grow one overnight. The need for performance dictates what you need to do.

3. Involve many people in the hiring process—especially peers and subordinates of the position being filled. You are looking for a fit that goes beyond a straight technical fit. You know who this new person will be working with; get them to help on the hiring. Retain the decision for yourself, but get others involved. This also helps the potential employee evaluate your organization and decide whether she wants to work here. The overall result is better fit and faster contribution to departmental performance. My success in hiring effective performers increases markedly when I involve others in the process.

4. See staff additions or changes as an opportunity to alter focus or direction or emphasis. An able new person with a unique set of skills can be very helpful in educating you and others on new horizons, challenges, or perspectives. Consider this as you decide what kind of person you want to bring in.

5. Write a "contract" between you and the new person. Not a legal contract, but (as some have called it) a psychological contract. In it list what you expect from each other and what you expect to give each other. Get agreement on these expectations before the individual has accepted the job. Use this loose contract as your initial working agreement and live

with it in operation for a few months before formalizing your expectations of each other in a performance plan. This will give the person enough time to get on board before making important performance commitments.

6. From the beginning, work with the person as you would expect to work with him later on. Right from the first interview, move responsibility to the individual. Expect the individual to initiate. Be open about concerns as well as challenges, fears as well as joys, problems as well as opportunities. Show him what it is like to work in your department by working with him from the start. This begins the process of building the independent, self-reliant staff professional you are seeking.

Your working professionals need at least four kinds of skills: technical, managerial, consulting, and interpersonal. You need to document more specifically what these skills are so staff members can assess themselves against what is needed and stop thinking of themselves in terms of technical skills only—which will not get the job done.

Staff skills

1. *Technical skills* include not only the skills needed by your staff to do their present work, but also related skills needed in your department outside their immediate responsibilities. Emphasizing these related skills shows that development is a departmental priority, increases intradepartmental understanding, and increases flexibility in terms of the resources you can bring to any situation. I would also include in these technical skills the ability to relate the skills to the business and a sound understanding of how the business works.

2. *Managerial skills* refer to the management of resources. For individuals this includes themselves, time, and information, at a minimum. It may also include equipment, materials, and money. Related skills are project management, time management, decision-making, and problem analysis. For the sake of sorting out managerial skills from the others, I imagine them as the more rational skills a person can exercise alone in her office. Not that managerial skills should be exercised alone, but the individual needs to be able to exercise them alone.

3. *Consulting skills* have to do with the process used to engage a customer on a project. From the initial meeting to the closing handshake, these skills are related to implementing the work with a customer department rather than the content of the work. The process is discussed at length earlier in this book.

4. *Interpersonal skills* include speaking, listening, supporting, confronting, managing conflict, empathizing, giving and receiving feedback, understanding, expressing feelings, disclosing. And the list goes on.

These skills are important to working with and living with others, and they can make the difference between success and failure on a project. I suggest that you build a list of your own and use success-failure as a criterion for including skills on your list. Organize it in whatever way is useful to you and your people. Assess yourself and others against this list—not as a performance appraisal, but as a development tool.

Staff development

Help your people think in terms of growing sideways as well as upwards in their jobs. Staff people are very familiar with the advantages of moving up. And up has limitations. In pyramidal structures it becomes less possible with each move. It only happens to us three or four times before we find ourselves in one job for a long time. So let's start looking at development within a job as an important opportunity and deal with upward movement more as the frosting than the cake.

A convenient rationalization? Perhaps. But look at all that you can do with a person now, in this job, when her attention is focussed on present development rather than future movement. You can build development into her objectives so she consciously grows through her work. You can identify the major competencies needed in jobs across your department and assess individuals against these competencies. You can provide regular training and development of the staff to help them learn. You can cross-train people. You can build vacation backups. And when you take these actions according to a plan, people will know that development, growing sideways in their jobs, is important to you. And they are more likely to stay for the developmental opportunity.

Management-by-objectives systems emphasize measurable results. Some coach the manager to keep his eye entirely on the result to be achieved, leaving the methods to the subordinate—she'll figure out how to get there. Development, on the other hand, has to do with how you get to the results. It is focussed on method, on the means to the end. To develop someone, you must pay attention to how she goes about doing the job. A developmental manager pays attention to both the results and the method of getting there when the subordinate is learning. After mastery of the methodology the manager does not need to give time to the steps leading to the outcome.

MBO and development

Permanent position plugs

Developing people means movement sideways and up, movement to new positions, new objectives, or new projects. You must retain the flexibility to do this. I was recently talking with a financial vice-president who was struggling to give developmental opportunities to his more junior supervisors. We looked at his organizational chart as we talked. Each time I would point to a position that perhaps could be vacated so someone else could make a developmental move into it, he would reply, "Oh, I can't do that. She's too good at that job to move her out. And where would I put her?" The message I got was that he had filled all his positions with an eye toward immediate performance and in doing so had lost the flexibility he needed to develop people. We eventually came up with some ideas for trades and cross-training, but the experience causes me to caution you: as you fill positions, keep staff development and job performance in mind. This will assure you of the performance you need tomorrow and keep you from blocking all of your positions today.

Performance and development

Too often we deal with what is expected on the job as distant from development of the performer. How often have you seen development plans for an individual with a primary focus on the workshops she will attend or the books he will read? As valuable as these off-site activities can be, they don't come close to replacing on-the-job experience as the primary way of developing staff.

Take it for granted that people are going to learn from their experiences, whatever those might be. As manager, your task is to set up the kind of experiences you want people to learn from, to point out the learning that is possible, and to follow up to see what happened. Put an individual's performance objectives against the skills she needs to perform competently in this job. When reviewing an individual's performance plans for the year, consider the developmental opportunities available to her in these plans; make sure they are there.

For example, when a staff member whose work has been analytical and solitary needs to improve formal communication skills, build management presentations into her objectives and action plans for the coming year. Or when another staff member seems caught up in the more immediate and tactical, put him on the task force working on the department's five-year plan—and give a more experienced member responsibility for helping him learn. Do not allow a performance plan to get by you without building in significant development opportunities for your staff. The challenge comes from the opportunity to learn something new while doing something important.

Independence

Develop your people to stand on their own—to represent the department. You need to have the confidence that they are working toward the same mission and strategy that you are. You need to know that their on-the-spot decisions are guided by the same philosophy and values that you espouse. You want to know that, no matter where you and they might be in the organization, you are all tuned into the same functional frequency.

This goal carries with it quite a different set of managerial behaviors than a goal that expects people to check in with you at every turn. It requires heavy involvement of your professionals in deciding the vision, mission, philosophy, values, strategy, structure, roles, responsibilities, goals, objectives, plans, methods, policies, and procedures of your department—that's all. To operate independently and in a manner that fits with what the department is and where it is going, they need to be involved in deciding those important issues. And this means lots of long meetings with groups and individuals which in turn means that your meeting skills had better be diverse and effective.

Managing the individual contributor

If you manage a group of individual contributors, they will on occasion question the need for you. They see their own work as paramount in importance and often view your interest in them or integration of their efforts as meddlesome. Their project focus conflicts with your department-direction focus. They are often better at telling you what they don't want than at telling you what might be done instead. This makes it difficult to manage.

Part of your dilemma is that you want your individual contributors to have room to operate on their own—and at the same time, you must be assured that they are moving in concert with departmental directions. Most of the guidance you give them in the here and now will be lost if it does not build on a common foundation established in departmental meetings. Not the weekly type, but the at least annual (and hopefully semiannual) two- or three-day meetings where the department takes a look at its direction and performance. With this foundation that they helped build, your daily efforts at aligning a wandering professional are more successful.

Reward and recognition

For those of us who manage in large organizations, discussions of reward for performance often center on the performance appraisal and salary administration systems—which do not appear to have much relationship to each other. You and I have spent much time talking about why our salary system doesn't really work and how little flexibility we managers really have to affect people's pay. Let's stop this gripe session right now by saying, "You are right. Now, how do you plan to reward your people for good performance?"

The answer is in soft rewards, not the hard reward of dollars. It is not a substitute for money; instead it is the daily departmental currency you trade in. It is up to you to increase the value of this currency, to up the exchange rate. Look at all the things you and your people want that you can control or influence: significance, responsibility, support, recognition, status, training, meaningful work, opportunity, challenge, risk, achievement, learning, control, authority, development, praise, criticism, power, independence, guidance, esteem, motivation, enthusiasm, excitement . . . the list is much longer, but you get the idea.

A staff department that does all of this is significantly different from one which seldom pursues these things. You can tell that the people enjoy coming to work and know they are in a unique setting. They are generous in their appreciation of each other, and they work hard because they want to. They mutually subscribe to some underlying ideals that support their belief that their work is important. If offered the opportunity to move to another company, all that they have in this department would cause them to think long and hard about making the move—and they would probably discuss the opportunity with their boss and coworkers. Their experience with the soft currencies of reward and recognition puts hard cash in perspective.

Special staff rewards

Let's elaborate on the special rewards that are more often achieved by staff people than by line:

1. *Wide exposure to the corporation*. Since staff functions serve so many people across the company, there is the opportunity for a company-wide perspective.

2. *Visibility*. When you compare grade levels, staff to line, you usually find that more staff people at lower levels have contact with executive levels.

3. *Time*. Many staff professionals operate without the time crunch their line counterparts experience.

4. *Planning*. Tied to time is planning. Many staff professionals are expected to plan for the future; it is part of their jobs.

5. *Individual contribution*. Though a staff person usually carries less responsibility, he usually has more opportunity to work a project through alone. Some of us see that as a reward of staff work.

6. *Specialization*. Though it can be narrowing, it can also be appealing. Line people who specialize don't have the opportunity to use what they have learned as widely as do staff people.

7. *Power*. Yes, it may be narrow and not the primary objective of the whole corporation, but there is power available to staff personnel in a narrow band of responsibility.

8. *Association with power*. Related to the last point and the earlier one on visibility, we do have the opportunity to associate occasionally with powerful people in the organization. To some of us it is important to be able to call the president by her first name.

These eight items are more than enough for me to find staff work rewarding. What else do you want?

All dressed up and nowhere to go

Staff functions, more than line functions, are made up of individuals more committed to their profession than the company. They look ahead at their future with this company and can see the path blocked—in effect, permanently—by a senior staff manager who will be in the blocking position long after the staff professional is qualified to move up. Where do they go? Elsewhere. Not because of any lack on the company's part that it can or should improve upon. It is just a fact of life for staff management. There are few organizations that can continue to provide that career mobility that many of your able and younger people want. So be prepared to "graduate" many of them.

The intent is not to encourage them to move on; in fact, you want them to stay longer. And you want to be able to plan your department's future, too. To this end, work at establishing an environment in which your people are more likely to talk with you about what their next career steps are likely to be. If you have the information that one of your better professionals is thinking about leaving, you can at least consider that possibility in your plans. And you might be able to affect her plans now that you know what they are. Try striking this deal with your people: if they are considering leaving, they should talk with you about it because you would like the chance to attempt to deal with their reasons for moving on. In return, if they do decide to seek other work, you will help them in that process. Since you have likely been around the field longer than they, there is a good chance you have contacts that they don't have. A deal like this can eliminate the surprise of a two-week notice. It gives you time both to consider how you might keep a valued employee and to plan on how to replace her.

Whenever you meet with subordinates, try to give them something that they find useful. It may be praise, it may be a new perspective, it may be responsibility, feedback, or the benefit of your experience. Establish a pattern of useful encounters with you—and "useful" is on their terms, as well as your own. This keeps them coming back to use you. And it does not keep you from getting what you want from these meetings also.

There are two areas in which you can contribute to them: content and process. You can add to what they know (content), or you can comment on how they work (process). Each is important. Whatever you do, try to do it in a way that allows them to leave your office feeling better than when they came in. Build their self-esteem.

An intent for staff managers

Managing Your Career

Overview

Here are four situations that many of us face in our careers:

- Starting up in staff management

- Moving into a new job

- Reshaping an old job

- Finding new meaning in an old job

These situations are unique enough to deserve separate chapters. The chapters provide the more focussed guidance you need when you find yourself in one of these four career positions.

Starting Up in Staff Management 30

We have all heard and told stories about excellent accountants, or PR people, or auditors, or lawyers who—because of their technical expertise—are rewarded with promotion to a managerial position. The one in the story usually turns out to be an abysmal manager; everybody agrees that he ought to go back to where he came from; nobody tells him about his problem or helps him with it; he punishes himself for not being a good manager and suffers daily with his management duties . . . and lives unhappily ever after.

Could this be you? Our preoccupation with our technical field does not suddenly depart when we are promoted to a managerial slot. Quite the contrary. The pressures to succeed in a new and unfamiliar position often lead to emphasizing those skills that got us the promotion. We continue to pursue projects without providing the direction, planning, systems, and leadership that come with our new managerial slot.

Our motivation for doing outstanding technical work for years probably wasn't because we wanted to become a manager. No, most of us did that good work because we loved it, or at least liked it, or maybe just felt it was important to do well. In any case, our re-

Could this be you?

cent work history has prepared us to keep doing what we have been doing—not to give it all up and step into the executive suite.

How important is management?

Here's a little test. Jot down the subjects of the last six articles or books you have read—those that relate to work. Now, how many of those articles or books were on technical subjects, related to the day-to-day work that you do? And how many of them were on management? What journals do you receive on a regular basis? How many of them are devoted primarily to management? Have you attended a workshop recently? Was its focus technical or managerial?

When you add up your score, what seems to dominate the development time you squeeze in around doing your job? For many staff managers the clear answer is keeping up with the technical side of their jobs. If this is true for you, imagine how it would be if you gave as much time to managerial reading and workshops as you do to technical matters. How does that sound to you? Common reactions I've heard include: "But I don't have that much time to give to learning about management." Or "I've got work to do!" These reactions are understandable, but they reinforce the technical orientation mentioned in the last paragraph.

Old skills block new

What is there in your skill repetoire that allowed you to perform especially well as an individual contributor? Is it possible that some of these same skills—which once served you so well— now stand in the way of effective managerial performance? For example, many of us learn early that if we want to excel individually, we must reduce our dependence on others to get the job done.

Most of our bosses prized (or at least said they prized) our ability to work unattended, to make decisions appropriate to our jobs, to search out potential problems and resolve them.

Those skills that allowed us to do so well now need to be put aside or overcome for us to do the managerial job we now need to do. It is one thing to work, decide, resolve problems independently; it is quite another to manage others who are doing the working, deciding, and resolving. Now we need to depend on them, to work interdependently. Now we need to make time and room for them to decide. Now we need to develop our staff's abilities to search out problems rather than do it ourselves. Put another way, now we need to unlearn many of those behaviors that made us so successful in the past.

Actually, it's more complicated than that. If we are not full-time managers, we have to do some of the technical work. So we have to decide when to manage, when to work, and when to use which skills. This is complicated!

S eeing others have difficulty with this move into management causes us to wonder about how we will do when we make the move. Do we have the talents to manage? Do we really want to manage? Or do we just want the added recognition, status, authority, power, money, and trappings of management?

Most of us have learned that we are supposed to want to manage. Our business school professors assumed it in the way they taught us. Our various bosses in the organization usually assumed that if we were smart, we would want a job like theirs—if not theirs. Discussions with peers often turned to our futures and the management ladder. Business literature has as heavy a bias toward upward mobility as popular advertising has toward sex appeal. Add to that a spouse, parents, and relatives who want you to be successful and you have a helluva lot of pressure to go after (and accept) that first management position.

But do I want it???

But do I want it??? My guess is that few of us slow down to ask this question. For many of us caught up in the business game at an early point in our careers and very achievement-oriented, if it is a prize of the game we'll take it. Our earlier success as a working professional supports our probable success in future efforts. So we take it.

But do I want it??? If it is early in your career; if you lack management experience; and if you are wondering whether you want to keep (or to take) this first management position, go for it! Try it, give it a chance long enough to really know what the job is, and then you can accept or reject it with the clear knowledge of your options. The alternative is to choose not to be a manager and to wonder what it would have been like to be one, whether we made the right choice. This wondering could continue for years—at least until the next time we are offered the same kind of opportunity. So my advice for those of you who after some consideration are still wondering whether you ought to be a manager is this: find out by being one for a while.

Changing frequencies

If you have never been a manager before, the initial experience of making the move from being an individual staff contributor is often quite jolting and disorienting. Staff professionals, more than line, get valued for their individual expertise, often unique in the whole organization. The move to management means giving up or using less of that expertise and beginning to use abilities that have been largely untested.

It is like you have been going through life listening to an AM radio. Your radio picks up the signals and translates them into sounds that you appreciate. One day, all of a sudden, your AM radio is taken away and you are given an FM Heathkit! Just a box of parts and no written instructions. Others around you with FM radios that they built for themselves give you advice on how to build yours. Often the advice is conflicting, and you notice that their FM radios don't work all that well. Some receive a very clear signal; others blare static; still others don't seem to pick up many signals. And with this kind of guidance and your lack of experience, you set about building a radio for yourself. It is trial and error all the way. Even before your radio is done, others are asking you what signals you are picking up and what you are learning from them. Nobody seems to have much sympathy for the fact that your radio isn't even together yet! If all goes well, you know that you, like some others, will be able to pick up signals both different from and of a higher quality than what you could get with your old AM receiver—if all goes well. In the meantime, you find yourself struggling to put this damned thing together! And wishing you still had your AM radio.

That is what moving into management the first time can be like. You are asked to give up what is familiar to you. You are asked to take on a job that no one describes very well to you. You are not given much day-to-day guidance. You are expected to perform. You are measured against criteria quite different from what was appropriate for you as an individual contributor. Your subordinates (who perhaps were your peers) have confusing expectations of you. Is it any wonder that you are tempted to withdraw, to protect yourself, or to flex your new authority muscles?

Moving into management gets recorded as one of those more important and difficult learning events in our lives on a par with basic military training, moving away from home, first love, or starting the first job. Surviving is an accomplishment; learning is different and painful. There is some consolation in the fact that many others have done it before you—and some have even managed to do it well. You can, too.

Moving into a New Job

31

H ere is the typical job selection process, which I have been through three or four times. After a number of interviews, they offer me the job. They spell out the salary, describe the job, show me where I will work, and tell me how enthusiastic they are about having me on the team. I accept the job. Then I go to work and find out what the job is really like.

For those of you who are saying "It's your own fault!"—you are right. I do need to take responsibility for not managing the process well. But this mistake is quite common. Too many of us rush through the "courtship" and end up in hasty "marriages." The haste in our process is brought about by the employer's need to fill the job quickly and her control of the job-filling process. Plus our need to be wanted, our desire to pursue opportunity, and our relative inexperience at going through a process like this.

Our experience reflects that many poor job marriages can be traced back to the courtship. Whether you were a partner in the marriage or just an observer of it, your retrospective insights often tell you, "We should have known that it wouldn't work." Some employers, recognizing the huge investment that rides on the selection decision, are beginning to do more about it. What can we, the potentially employed, do about it?

Negotiate your new job before you accept it

1. Write down, step by step, what the hiring process is for you.

2. Tell prospective employers about your process, at appropriate points and before important decisions have been made or assumed by them.

3. Find out how effectively your function is operating in another company. Put another way, what would you ask to find out how effective the department is? And who would you need to talk to? Write all this down on less than one page so you could explain it in less than five minutes.

4. What would your ideal job contain? If you could have any job you wanted—and still have a job—what would it include? List these thoughts and dream a little. Think about freedom, control, responsibilities, contacts, authority, professional support, relationships, rewards, recognition, accomplishment, power, work environment, fringe benefits, outside activities, work hours, location time at home, perquisites, travel, impact on family, promotional opportunities, work norms, organizational culture, the way in which you are managed, the social side of the job, office decor, incentives, and anything else that you want to include in this ideal work dream. Go back over the list and note those things that are particularly attractive to you, that you *really* want. Prioritize the list quickly (not because it isn't important, but because the basic intent is to cause you to think it through, not to analyze in depth). That's it. And what have you got? A much better and more current reading on what is really important to you in your work, unencumbered with all those practical considerations that you and prospective employers heap on you in the midst of the courtship-rush-to-marriage process.

5. Go back to the hiring process you described earlier. What are your high work priorities within your hiring process? How can you build them into your diagnosis of the organization as a place for you to work?

6. Insist on interviews with people you would have regular or important contact with, including peers, subordinates,

customers, and top management. Ask that they not only talk with you but be included in the selection process. In other words, it is not just an interview for your information; they are advising on the decision as to whether you get an offer or not. You want your coworkers to have a stake in selecting you. You want people to say "I helped pick her and I support her" rather than "I have to work with her because she was hired to do that job." What if they don't support you and you don't get the job you wanted? If a significant number of them advise "no," then maybe you have just been saved from a whole lot of trouble. If they advise "no" and you still get the offer, you are in a better position to deal with their opinion because it is known rather than never sought and unknown.

The attention I am giving to this job-picking process demonstrates its importance to me. You will be in this job for a long time; it will be very focal in your life; it deserves to be managed.

There is a point most of us face three to five times in our careers when we are very powerful—and it often goes by us unrecognized. That is the time between being offered a new position and accepting it. It is that time during which we are both wanted and uncommitted. Too often our own need for acceptance, or our excitement about the position, or our security needs cause us to move throughout this powerful career moment without acknowledging that it existed.

This is usually a time preceded by much thought about what we want out of our lives and careers. The job being offered is in response to something we have pursued (or maybe it is pursuing us). This is a time when we are relatively ignorant of what it will be like to work in the organization which wants us. Put another way, this is an ideal time to ask for whatever we want because we are too ignorant to be blamed and too attractive to ignore.

A power point

If we ask for something stupid, we can be excused. Ask for the same thing six months after accepting the job and we would be judged negatively—we ought to know better by then. So now is the time to ask and to be willing to accept no less than what we want as a reasonable answer. Chances are, if we don't ask now, it will be a long time before we will be in this powerful position again.

So figure out what you want. Is it access to higher management? To be appraised on a regular basis? More money? Vacation time in keeping with your professional experience? Wider responsibilities? An addition to your staff? A corner office? To report to a management committee? Higher dollar approval levels? What do you want?

Show your work through the interview process

Present yourself during the hiring process as you would present yourself at work. Use your same analytical frameworks, same line of questioning, and same style that you would later use on the job. Give those people considering you the feeling that they are working with you right now rather than considering you for work. The result is that they have a truer sense of who you are and what you bring to the job. Here are two examples.

A purchasing department manager had great success in improving the performance of his function for the company. Partly as a result of hearing of his success, another company contacted him, asking to interview him for their top purchasing job. In preparation for the interview, the manager reviewed the changes he had made in his own department and isolated eight key questions that allowed him to diagnose how the department was functioning. In the interviews with the interested company, he used these questions to understand (diagnose) how their purchasing function was operating—and he told them that he was doing this. This affected how he was seen, whom he talked with, how he understood this prospective employer, and how he presented himself. It gave him the initiative in the interviews as he moved through his structure. And it impressed the hell out of them! Through his diagnosis, he learned enough about their purchasing function to decide that he did not want the job they offered to him, and he felt very comfortable turning down the "opportunity."

A oil industry training supervisor was off at a workshop on organizational diagnosis. While there, she met a line manager from a drug company; he was attending because the models used in the workshop were being used back in his company. The line manager, impressed with the training supervisor, arranged to have her considered for the management development director slot in his company. In the interviews, she used the organizational model learned at the workshop and already in use at the drug company to develop questions she could ask her prospective employers. This resulted in a quick diagnostic look at the company, which she presented and verified with them before beginning to negotiate the terms of employment. She ended up accepting a job through having used a method that demonstrated to them how she worked.

Each of these examples differs from the typical hiring process in many ways. First of all, real work is done—and done in ways that fit with what would be expected of the candidates after they moved into their positions. Secondly, the candidates took the initiative and asked the prospective employers to think in their terms. This did not preclude the employers from also thinking in their own terms. Third, the candidates' processes reflected how they think about their staff function. They were in effect saying, "The questions I ask will tell you what is important to me and how I go about getting that information." Rather than "Ask me questions and I will answer them. This is how to find out about how I work." Notice the strong difference in those two stances and imagine how different the interviews might be.

You want to deliver on all you said you could do. Yes, you have an image to uphold. You want to show the company that you know how to work on their terms. You were hired to revolutionize the way this staff function delivers its services.

Your first month: don't do much—yet

But add these facts to the list: you just got here and you really don't know where "here" is. Your need to perform is outrunning your knowledge of the organization. People working around you are going to see quick action as precipitous. You are ignorant. So find out what is going on before you begin to change things. Here are some steps for orienting yourself:

1. Pursue in greater depth the diagnosis you made before coming to work here.

2. Listen to people tell you about how they do things (and how they don't do things around here). Deal with all this information quite respectfully.

3. Ask questions. Show that you understand the answers.

4. Empathize with people's situations; show that you understand their feelings.

5. Remember that you do not have to agree or disagree at this point. You *may* agree or disagree, but you do not have to. You are learning.

6. Take notes. The risk is that your learning from your earlier discussions will be lost in content and perspective in relation to what you have heard more recently. Approach this professionally; respect what people have to say by writing it down.

. . . but I need to do something!

Of course the organizational realities also dictate that something must be done. The department was operating before you got here, and its day-to-day decisions must still be made—probably even more so if the position has been vacant a while before your arrival. So how do you handle these immediacies?

Build yourself a warm-up and practice period that includes these objectives:

- During the next five weeks, I am going to be learning about this company and my function within it. That will be my priority.

- To this end, I will interview these people (list them), asking these questions (list them).

- At the end of this time, I will report in person and writing to these people (list them) on what I have learned, what I recommend, what I want to do, and how they can help.

- In the meantime, I will make the necessary and important daily decisions that come with my position, knowing that my later conclusions and recommendations could move me in quite different directions.

- In making these daily decisions, I will attempt to act in keeping with what has happened in the past insofar as that seems immediately advantageous to the company.

- I will attempt *not* to initiate new programs until the end of my learning and diagnostic period.

Make sense? You would no doubt express it a little differently in your organization, but the intent is pretty clear: expect a lot of me, but not immediately.

I can already feel you pulling back from that word "ignorance." It represents so much of what we do not want to be and so much of what we are as we move into a new position. This may be especially true of staff managers. Our new corporate-wide responsibilities involve interfacing with many managers, establish-

Build on your ignorance

ing relationships with each of those individual personalities, and representing our function to each of these diverse perspectives.

But back to building on your ignorance. Here are some ways to turn this liability to your advantage:

1. First of all, recognize that your ignorance is legitimate—at least for the first few months. Don't blame yourself and know that most others won't blame you, either. Accept it as real and innocent.

2. Next, proclaim it! Not in the boardroom perhaps, but to your boss, your staff, and your important contacts within the organization. It goes something like, "I am new around here and have an awful lot to learn." They will agree, appreciating your humility (and your profound insight).

3. Follow this statement with "I need your help getting up to speed. You know what I need to know. What's the best way for me to learn what is important in your realm?" This shows people that you think they are important, that you want to take action, and that you want to be influenced by them— all important points.

4. Now, schedule it. Follow your self-revelation with a declared and businesslike way of moving you out of ignorance and into organizational enlightenment.

5. Next, do it. Hold the meetings, collect and analyze the data, and report back to people who contributed to moving you to your more educated perspective on the organization. And do not miss this opportunity to continue the relationship you initiated by securing their assistance in doing what you have recommended.

Someone once told me that moving into a new job and charting one's feelings through time would look something like this:

Yes, it does resemble the square root sign. First, there is employment followed by the elation that comes with being on a new job, not knowing much about it, and not being responsible for delivering a lot immediately. This positive plateau is supported by being in a learning mode as you find out what is really going on in the organization. As your knowledge increases, time passes, and your need to act converges with others' expectations that you will act, you begin a deep dive into doubt, fear, anxiety, despair, confusion, hesitation, frustration—pick any two words that apply to you. This is when you reach the depths.

This is usually (unfortunately, not always) followed by an image of what can be done that allows you to provide the leadership and direction that the function needs. Besides the personal integration, you have the management support you need to move ahead. You know what you want to do in both the longer and shorter term. People are beginning to deal with you as a reality, as a part of the organization. You are beginning to develop some professional friends. All of these go to building, as the illustration suggests, a deeper and more positive feeling than you started out with—but only after risking what might have looked like career disaster a few months earlier.

Reshaping an Old Job 32

What do you do if you have been in your present position for a long time and you want to stay in it, but on different terms? First of all, read the chapters related to moving into a new job; that is good guidance on rethinking your old job.

It is easy to put off a consideration of what you presently have and what you want. How do you get started? Take advantage of corporate events and make them catalysts for rethinking your job. Some examples:

- It is strategic planning time for the department, and this has caused you to begin thinking about your role as manager.

- It is annual plan time, and this has caused you to begin thinking about what you really want to do.

- You just got back from a management development workshop that caused you to think about your job.

- You just finished a two-day off-site meeting with your top team, and you all agreed you should rethink your role as manager.

- You just had a performance discussion with your boss, and it seems useful to rethink your role.

- You just read a very helpful book on staff leadership that caused you to think about your role.

- As part of your objectives for this calendar year, you are going to redefine and renegotiate your role with your boss.

- The recent restructuring of the organization has caused you to think about how you can best respond to what the organization needs.

The length of this list suggests that there are numerous organizational events that can be used as the excuse to do what you want to do anyway. They just give you a business-related basis for action.

The psychological contract

An important communication and motivational tool available to all of us and used by a few is something called "the psychological contract." It has to do with the deal that is struck between a person and the organization she works for—what they expect of each other. Unlike legal contracts, this deal is usually implicit and undocumented. It also changes a lot through time, so it needs to be examined regularly. The contract can be applied to anyone who works in an organization. First, think about how clear your contract with the organization is right now. Is your boss aware of what you offer and expect in return? How clear are you on what you will give and get from the organization? What do either of you have in writing that supports the psychological contract that exists between you? Get it written down so you will not forget, and also so you can alter it in the future.

This contract gets to the heart of what you've got and what you want. Use it as the foundation for renegotiating your job. (Shown simply, it looks something like this:)

You have useful intuitive and analytical skills for working with your staff, your boss, your clients; it's time to turn these skills on yourself—with significant input from others. Change goes more smoothly when the people affected are involved and when the change you are about to make is a significant one. Locking yourself in your office and deciding what you want to be when you grow up will not give you the kind of support you need outside your office. A major shift in how you do your job requires major support. How do you do it? Here are ten steps for diagnosing yourself:

Diagnosing yourself

1. Think through what you want the job to be in the best of all possible worlds. If you could have everything you wanted in *this* job, what would it contain? How would you behave? How would others behave toward you? What would you be responsible for? How would you be measured? How

would you work with significant others in the organization? Who would the significant others be? How would you spend your time at work?

2. List people who know you and your job and whom you want to talk to about yourself. Include in the list significant contacts inside and outside the organization: your subordinates, boss, peers, spouse, clients, close friends, children, professional associates. The list should include people who care about you, people who will need to support your eventual decision with their own actions, people in positions of significant authority or influence, people who have expertise in helping others look at their careers. How many you list depends on the number who might actually be helpful, your investment in the project, the time you have available, and the time they have available. For now, think in terms of spending from thirty to sixty minutes with each person; this might help you decide how many to contact.

3. Write down the questions you want them to answer. You are going to be interviewing each of them and want to make sure that you ask each person to consider the same points, each from their own perspective. You will probably end up with a handful of questions, each rather open-ended, leaving room for the person to make her own unique response. The questions might be preceded with an introduction that sounds like this: "Because of (see reason list above), I am in the process of rethinking my role and responsibilities here at ABC Company, and I want your help. I am talking to a number of people important to me in performance of this job and asking each of them a few questions. After I have talked to everybody by (date), I will pull those ideas together with my own and write up a description of how I think this job should be approached in the future. I will talk with you about that; ask for your refinements of it; and ask for your active support of what I eventually decide upon. How does that sound to you?"

Given the individual's comfort with this approach, you could then go on to ask questions like:

- If you were to redesign what I do so that I would be of more aid to you, what would you retain, add to, or take away from the job?

- What will you be expecting of me in the future that you do not expect now? And what will you no longer expect that you *do* expect now?

- What are the most important parts of my job as you see it? The least important parts? How well do I cover those parts now?

- Assume we were starting from scratch and could design my job in any way we wanted. What do you think should be included in that design?

- What questions should I be asking you and others about how I do and should do my job?

4. Interview each person and write down what they say. Check with them to make sure that you understand. Writing it down causes you to pay more attention, shows them that this is important to you, and helps you remember. Try to complete all of your interviews within two weeks because the forgetting curve will take over and swallow much of your data with it. Be quiet during the interviews. Let your questions speak for themselves. You may even find it useful to just put the written questions before the person and ask him to talk while you write. Remember that while you are talking you are not learning anything and are probably biasing the responses you are getting. Shutting up is one of the hardest things for us to do. Your responses are best confined to showing that you understand what the person means; agreement is not implied. Many managers find it useful to talk with their subordinates in a group. Or perhaps give them a group task that involves reaching consensus on the answers to your questions. Tell people when you will get back to them and with what.

5. Review the psychological contract you were hired under. Why did they bring you to the organization? What difference do they expect you to make? Who are "they"? What does the old job description say? How accurate is it? How invested are others in it? Write down the more important points.

6. Analyze and explore the data intuitively. You have at least three sources of data (two of which we have discussed): what you want the job to be (step 1); what others want it to be (step 4); and what the job has been (step 5). After shuffling through all that you have heard from yourself and others, search out the patterns (and lack of patterns) in what you have heard. Do this in a more logical fashion initially, leaving room from the more illogical and important intuitive part as well. By all means, emphasize any intuitions, gut feelings, glimmers, or other less reasonable insights that come to you. You are, after all, working on defining a part of you, not a machine. So the product will not look like or read like a machine (except to the extent that you are machine like).

7. Describe your job—as you propose it should be. Based on what you have heard from your inner self, your experience, and your interviews with others, what do you propose to do in this position in the future? As you write the description, keep these points in mind:

   • Get it down on less than two typed (double-spaced) pages.

   • Write it so that what you want to do in this position clearly shows through.

   • Write it in a way that communicates to others in the organization, that fits with the norms and style of written communication. You want their support of this.

   • Emphasize how this role, these actions, will benefit the organization.

- Do not emphasize how this is different from what you have been doing. Do not write about what your job was versus how it should be. Instead, focus on how this approach serves the organization.

- Do not follow the Personnel Department approach to writing job descriptions unless that is likely to increase others' understanding and support.

- Write so that readers of your words know that you said this, you believe it, and you want it.

8. Test your proposal on others. The best way to do this is to make a short appointment, give it to them to read, and note their reactions. Give it to them expecting to hear some suggestions; welcome any you get. Notice where your proposal is not clear. Expect to polish it. You may want to try it out on some trusted and knowledgeable few before moving on to important others. This would give you a chance to revise it. In the reactions you get, look for support. Is this person likely to help you in carrying out these new notions about how you will do your job? Do not be too dismayed at hesitation; you can get some comfort from the fact that there are people who don't like your old approach to the job so it is not surprising that some will not favor your new approach. In the end, it is your job, and you must feel that it meets your needs and the organization's.

9. Recommend the necessary changes in the job and begin action. You have given ample opportunity to influence all of the important parties. It is time to put something in final form.Tell others that you have heard them and understand them, that this is what you want to do, and that you want their support. Getting their acceptance is usually easier than moving that acceptance to action. When you reshape your job, others have to reshape the way they work with you, and that is uncomfortable. It is especially not easy for you because you have all these new relationships to deal with.

But it is also hard for each of the others because they didn't initiate this change; they will vary in their enthusiasm for supporting it, regardless of how much groundwork you have laid.

10. Follow through and follow up. This is where the persistence comes in. This is the hardest part because the excitement of exploring and deciding is finished and now you have to make the changes stick. You stand to benefit from this. So *you* must make it work. If you can, set it up so you are appraised on how well you make it work. That being the case, you have succeeded in making it important to the organization for you to do this. This also assures that your boss will be following up in some way on what you are doing. Here are other actions you can take:

- Ask how you are doing. Ask your boss, your subordinates, your clients, whoever may notice. Asking gives you data and causes them to think again about the changes you are making.

- Tell others how you are doing. Give them regular reports on how you are progressing with the changes you are making.

- Update the description. You will learn more about what you should do as you begin to carry out the described role. Use this learning to keep your job description alive. Your goal is not to write it in stone and stash it away; quite the opposite.

- Reinforce others for the help they continue to give. This also reminds them of your newly conceived and now executed role. Continue to expect this support, because it is for the good of the organization.

Diagnosing yourself often leads to diagnosing the organization. How can a staff department manager take a serious look at how she carries out that role without looking at the rest of her organization? The identification of the manager with the function means that you cannot mess with one without messing with the other. True, but maybe you haven't got the time to do it all right now. Or maybe you look at your role in preparation for rethinking the departmental role. Or vice versa. You will figure out your own reasons and priorities. I do know that it is possible to focus on the staff manager and on restructuring that role—and to do this as a starting point. But have no doubt, it will stir many other issues in the organization.

Diagnosing your organization

Finding New Meaning in an Old Job

33

Recapturing your job's lost meaning

Why do you keep doing this? "It's a job . . . I like the people . . . I need the money . . . It's not so bad . . . It has meaning to me." No, really, *why*? Let's explore why you are in this job and in this kind of work. This deserves thinking about no matter what your present experience with the job is—you do not just wait for the bad times to move in before stopping to think about the meaning of work in your life. Bad times force that consideration as serious illness forces larger life considerations, but it is unfortunate if the only time we think about life is when we are threatened with losing it. So it is with our work as a part of our life. We need to think about it from time to time.

I am going to suggest a rather personal consideration of how work fits into your life and adds to your life's meaning. This means starting with larger life purposes and issues, and then seeing how being a staff manager fits into that larger picture. Some of you will experience this section of the book as its most useful contribution to you, and others will wonder all the way through it what this has to do with being a staff manager. Your reactions to this section might themselves be some indication of where you are in terms of thinking about the work-life relationship.

The life-work/ work-life relationship

In the next few pages we are going to explore how your life work fits with your work life. "Life work" means what you have set out to do in your allotted years on this planet. "Work life" means how things are going at the office. You've heard "How's your love life?" Well, this is "How's your work life?" The relationship between life work and work life can best be explored by clarifying each of them. And we'll start with the big one, life work. Consider these questions:

- If you are on a journey, where are you going?

- If you were to paint a picture of your destination, what would it look like?

- If you were to describe what you hope to see along the way, what would you include?

- What difference do you hope to make in this world? What do you want out of life?

- What is truly important in this life?

Each of these questions is posed from a life perspective (so pull yourselves away from that staff job for a while). The questions are familiar enough to some of us; the answers, and the process for reaching the answers, are not as familiar. Knowing that, I want you to work on the questions and answers.

1. Go through the questions listed above and select one that fits with your way of thinking about life and its meaning. Answer it. That process will be aided by a pencil and paper and at least sixty minutes of thinking time in a quiet room, alone. (Just having this time is enough to make this whole effort worthwhile for the more harried readers.) Let yourself write down whatever thoughts come to mind about the questions you choose. And don't try to make sense out of all this too early. You can always go back and organize and tidy up and improve on what you've said. Just jot down words

as they randomly cross your mind. Some of you may find it more helpful to draw pictures of what you "see" than to describe it in words.

As you work, sit back and relax. This is not a task that calls for a college exam approach. Know that whatever you write down is correct. The only way to get this "wrong" is to try to do it "right." You are the only person who will be reading what you write. Don't read further in this book until what you have written *adequately* (not perfectly) portrays the larger life meaning that you want to move toward.

2. When you are through, you may have two or three sheets in front of you which started off rather unfocussed and tentative, words written apparently at random. Further down the page(s), the content comes into clearer focus and begins to sort out, priorities become clearer, phrases and sentences begin to form, a larger meaning begins to emerge. On the other hand, you may have approached this task thoughtfully but more directly, moving immediately into writing clear, complete sentences expressing your answers to the questions you selected. Whatever approach you took, you came up with a written product and some feelings about that product and the time you spent on it.

Now look at your high priorities. How specific are they? How measurable? How achievable? Most of the time they are not specific, cannot be measured, and cannot be achieved in any permanent sense—and that is wonderful! Yes, this is a time when our customary guidance about goals and objectives goes out the window. Life purposes transcend measurability in the normal, day-to-day sense we are used to.

3. Review what you have written, looking for anything that is achievable in a definite time frame (like making so much a year or owning a piece of property) and ask yourself why you want that. See if it ties into something else on your list that is less measurable (like security or happiness). If it does, indicate this on what you have written.

4. Life work has to do with reaching for a vision of how things

could be. It has to do with striving to accomplish some ideals—like those you wrote about. The ideals are always just beyond our grasp, enticing in their perfection and impossible to hold on to for very long. Happiness frequently appears among people's life-work goals. I am happy today, but I do not have a headlock on happiness. It has escaped me before and will escape again. It is not like buying a new car. Look at what you have written and see how much of it is as elusive as happiness versus how much is measurable and attainable. With circles or underlining, sort out the more elusive from the more attainable life purposes.

5. Enough on the content for now; let's talk about your feelings about doing this. How would you describe them? Comfortable? Uncomfortable? Impatient? Anxious? Confused? Calm? Uncertain? Empty? Confident? Irritated? Exhilarated? What feelings could you add? The way you feel is at least partially related to how much you think about these life-work issues. Someone who has not thought about these matters for five years is going to deal with them much differently than someone who has just returned from a career-planning workshop. The feelings are worth looking at because they may be saying something to you about the relevance of this kind of thinking to your life's work. Those of you who feel comfortable, patient, confident during the writing period likely find that the process reinforces the directions you are moving in. Those of you who feel quite the opposite likely question the approach and are struggling to see its relevance to being an effective staff manager. Notice how your feelings relate to the content you wrote.

6. Before moving on to work life, recognize that there is nothing more important to a staff manager than having clarity about what is important in this life. Knowing, and living by, the answers that you wrote will give you more self-assurance, balance, and sense of what to do than you can learn in any management or technical workshop. Believe your answers and put them before you daily. They will give you the confidence to risk more because you know what the important

things in this life are. You will have aligned yourself with values and ideals that transcend the work place and give you the power of a larger perspective that is more important to you. Living by what you believe empowers you.

7. How does your work life fit into your life work? Use as a starting point all that you have written about what you want out of life. What has your work got to do with it? Go back over the pages you wrote earlier and (with a different-colored pen) mark each of those important areas in which your work life contributes significantly. For now, do not worry about the quality of contribution; instead pay attention to the quantity. "My work contributes a lot toward my need for growth." Got the idea? Go over what you have written and mark it.

8. Notice how many marks you have made. They give you some indication of whether your work is important to what you want out of life. The person with few marks is certainly in quite a different position regarding her work than the person with many—though the reasons would not be clear to us. I feel safe in saying that if you do not have many ways in which your work is contributing to your life work, then you'd better have something else damned important going on outside those fifty plus hours per week that you spend working. You may be able to accept less meaning from work and live with it. But the staff manager who does not find potential satisfaction for life goals through work will, in all likelihood, not be very good at it. So those of you who found yourselves underlining much of what you wrote about your life work, take heart. And those with less underlining, take note.

9. Now that we have noted the quantities, it is time to consider the quality of support for life work that your job offers. Find that one item in the description of what you are reaching for in this life that your work contributes the most to. Put a circled "1" beside it. Also indicate the items that deserve a "2" and "3." Now, on a separate sheet of paper, write down examples of things your work has allowed you

to do that moves you toward what you most want out of life (item 1). List as many as come to mind; list them quickly and in shorthand fashion—the purpose here is to build awareness, not to be elaborate. When you start running out, move on to item 2 and do the same thing, and then item 3 and so on until you feel you have done a good job of noting the various ways in which your work helps you get what you want out of life.

10. Some of you probably got here much faster than others. Those of you who did not have much to write might consider changing this job, leaving this job, or giving more time outside the job to activities that give you more life satisfaction. Some lists express indirect contributions of work to life goals. For example, "My work provides me with money and vacation. That allows me to travel. Travel allows me to learn and grow, which allows me to reach my potential, which is important in my life's work." It is clear that the nature of your work is not necessarily important; it's the money and time off that are important. Contrast that statement with this one: "My work provides me with the opportunity to learn from other people, which allows me to reach my potential as a human being, which is important in my life's work." Notice the difference. Effective staff managers have more direct connections between what they want out of life and their work. This is evident not just through building lists, but to the people working around them.

11. So now what do you do? Regardless of how much your work life serves your life's work, the basic task is to make it serve even more. There are a number of ways for doing this:

    • Change your perception of what is important to you in life so that it better fits with your job. This is very difficult but not impossible. It happens naturally throughout life; some of us push the process with rationalizing to justify our immediate situation.

    • Change jobs, moving to one that better fits what you want out of life. Again, difficult but not impossible.

- Change this job so that it includes more of what you want out of life. An earlier chapter of this book talks about just such a process.

- Change your perception of the job so you realize all the things it is or can be, giving you that fit with what you want out of life. Possible, though you risk rationalization.

- Change the amount of energy you put into work. Reduce it as much as possible so you have more available for life priorities outside of work. This has been done many times. It works, but if you have accepted the challenge of the quest, it's not for you.

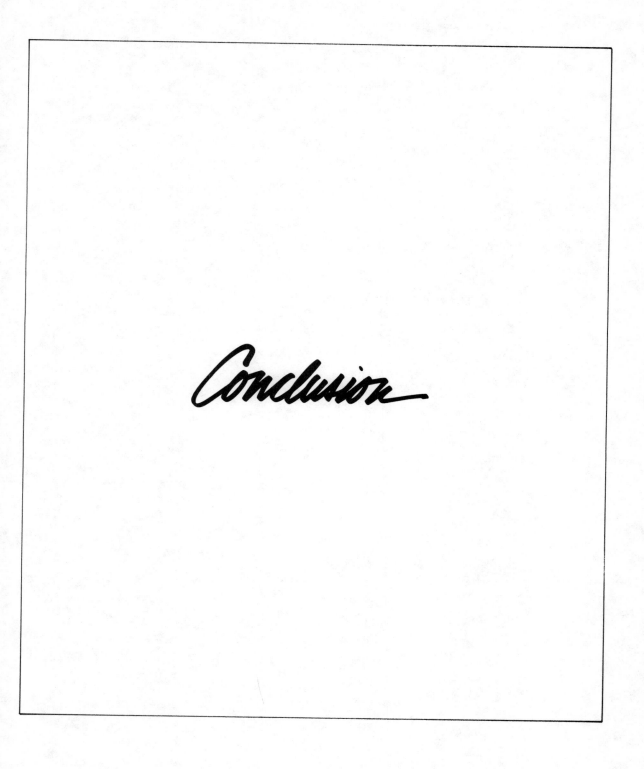

Conclusion

Making Personal Changes

34

Since you have been pursuing this quest for staff leadership with the hope that you can use it to create changes in your work, here is one way of looking at change:

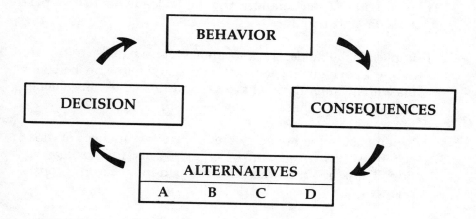

The model illustrates the idea that there are certain consequences to behavior that could be viewed as positive or negative. To the extent that the consequences are more positive, I will probably want to continue in my behavior. To the extent that the consequences are more negative, I will probably be more open to changing my behavior because it is not getting me what I want. In either case, positive or negative, I have a range of alternative behaviors to choose from. Based on the consequences, I will decide on a behavior for next time. If behavior A isn't working so well, I am more likely to substitute behavior B and see what its consequences are. And so the cycle goes.

You can think of the model in relation to what you have read in this book. The book causes you to consider your present behavior and its consequences. To the extent you find the book reinforcing, you are more likely to continue doing what has worked in the past. If the book helps you realize some negative consequences you hadn't thought of before, you will be a bit more open to alternatives to your present behavior. That could lead you to deciding on a different alternative for the next time.

The model (and the book) put the responsibility with you to decide what is best for you—what yields the best consequences. The book guides your self-awareness and consideration of consequences. It provides you with alternatives as well as ways of making the decision. But the book (and the model) cannot tell you what is right, what to choose.

There are other considerations the model leads me to as a person and as a staff manager:

1. Implicit in the model is self-awareness. I have to be very aware of how I am behaving as a staff manager, of how my behavior fits with my intentions. I have to know how to use my abilities and know my limitations.

2. When I act, I need to be aware of the consequences of those actions within myself, with other people, and for the organization. Think about all the skills implied in measuring consequences of your managerial behavior:

   • Understanding of others' reactions, awareness of nonverbal behavior.

   • Ability to ask how your behavior is affecting others.

- Ability to listen to the response.

- Understanding of other people's values.

- Acceptance of those values.

- Knowledge of your own feelings and how those feelings are impacted by what you are doing.

- Ability to set up feedback systems that provide you information on consequences. Measuring consequences of behavior involves a receptive set of skills that goes beyond what the model might initially imply.

3. As discussed above, our managerial actions have consequences. So does the way we view our actions and our lives. Believing that I know a lot, that I can make a difference, that I am in charge, obviously affects the way I meet the world. It shows, and, more important, it feels different to me. I will notice different details, events, interactions, comments. I will listen, respond, relate differently because of this perspective. As a consequence of adopting this perspective, I have more alternatives in my life, I make more choices, I am more aware of being responsible for what happens to me.

4. If I am aware of my behavior and the consequences of it, I have a considerable set of skills! Self-confident and effective managers usually have this winning combination. They are self-aware without being self-conscious, and they pay attention to the impact of what they do and adjust—which leads to the next point.

5. To adjust, I need viable alternatives. When I think that I am doing my very best, but it isn't working and I don't have anything else I can do, I am in trouble!! I need options! Much of my development as a manager is about increasing my options. Successful managers have many actions they *could* take, and this increases their confidence in the action they eventually *will* take.

6. When looking at "alternatives" in terms of ability, I see that I need to be a very receptive manager, open to many ways of accomplishing a task. More than receptive, I need to be actively seeking various ways of doing this job. This means talking with others about it—even when I don't have any problems. This means reading books and articles that allow others to share their alternatives with me. This means actively discussing with others involved what I might do before I do anything. Now that is quite a different manager from the one whose mind is set on alternative A, does not see alternatives B, C, or D, and stubbornly moves ahead with what really is the only way he knows.

7. The alternatives piece of the model is rich with possibilities and one we too frequently gloss over quickly as we move to deciding on what our behavior will be. The main skills required to develop alternatives rely on creativity, patience, and a willingness to withhold a need to control. We need to be good question-askers, good listeners, and especially good at allowing time for encouraging new alternatives to surface. If, during all of this, we remind ourselves that in the end we control what we will do—and that decision will be better for having explored the alternatives—then we are able to contribute more freely in the alternative-generating process.

8. Deciding among alternatives requires skills typically related to decision-making. We have to weigh the outcomes we expect as a result of this decision, clarifying what is more and less important to us, what we "must" have and what we "want" to have in the resultant behavior. Many of those musts and wants can be related to the consequences we desire. Making the decision is a combination of rational and intuitive forces brought together in a solid outcome. My own perspective, when I am trying to decide what to do, is to weigh my alternatives rather objectively, pick the one that makes the most sense, and then do what I really want to do! This can mean that the decision I logically selected, since it is supported by my gut feeling as well as logic, becomes the obvious choice. On the other hand, it is equally possible that my objective

choice is not supported by what my gut or intuition tells me and results in my choosing an alternative different from what logic would dictate.

9. This is a delicate point for those of us who find ourselves closer to either end of the rational-emotional spectrum in decision-making. For you who are more rational, introducing a strong emotional element in the process seems antithetical. For you more emotionally based deciders, making too much sense out of it is a major concern. The people at the ends of the spectrum have something to learn from each other. Emotion can enrich logic. And logic can inform emotionally based decisions. To routinely decide from either end of the spectrum is a mistake.

A manager needs a way of deciding on her behavior that considers both what logic says she should do and emotion tells her she wants to do. The behavior resulting from the decision needs a rationale and commitment behind it. Rationale does not flow out of emotion. Commitment does not flow out of logic. For our behaviors to represent us well, they need to be an integrated product of what our head, heart, and gut are telling us. Then we can move forward with confidence.

The never-ending quest

It is difficult to end a book that has no conclusion. No one gets saved in the last chapter. No ". . . and they lived happily ever after." No solving of the mystery and tying up of the loose ends. The quest to become a staff leader continues. It does not end when you close the covers of this book. I have tried to provide some ways to plan and plot your route and to note your progress. But, as most of us have found, the destination always appears as a glow just over the horizon, and there is no direct path to it.

In our search for ways of expressing ourselves through our life work, we are not likely to find "the way." Seeking answers throughout our careers and our lives moves us always closer to the ideals we envision, yet somehow we never arrive. We can take this fact as either a source of constant frustration or a call to search further and deeper.

We need to appreciate that the meaning is as much in the questing as in the arriving. In striving to become leaders in our organizations, we grow. In risking new approaches to staff management, we become stronger. In expressing ourselves through our work, we realize more of our potential. Growing, becoming, and realizing are all ongoing, expanding processes. and such is the nature of the quest.

Resources

Bell, Chip R. *Influencing: Marketing the Ideas That Matter*. San Diego: Learning Concepts, distributed by University Associates, 1982. Thoughts on getting things done in organizations; especially appropriate for staff. Bell offers workshops.

Bennis, Warren, and Burt Nanus. *Leaders: The Strategies for Taking Charge*. New York: Harper & Row, 1985. Identifies key leadership abilities based on a study of ninety executives. Thought-provoking.

Block, Peter. *Flawless Consulting*. San Diego: Learning Concepts, distributed by University Associates, 1981. Another perspective on how staff professionals consult. Many practical ideas. Block offers workshops.

Boyatzis, Richard E. *The Competent Manager*. New York: John Wiley & Sons, 1982. Years of research support this view of what managers actually do and what the basis for managerial effectiveness is.

Cuming, Pamela. *The Power Handbook*. Boston: CBI Publishing Co., Inc., 1981. Powerful thoughts and exercises that expand your range of alternatives.

Drucker, Peter F. *Management: Tasks, Responsibilities, Practices*. New York: Harper & Row, 1973. The Bible. Not for reading cover to cover, but in pieces, using the excellent index. Look up his views on staff and support.

Fear, Richard A. *The Evaluation Interview*. New York: McGraw-Hill, 1978. A rather traditional and useful approach to gathering information. Helpful in many one-on-one situations.

Herman, Stanley M., and Michael Korenich. *Authentic Management*. Reading, Massachusetts: Addison-Wesley, 1977. Quite a different perspective on managing yourself and your work based on Gestalt theory. Empowering for many.

Kanter, Rosabeth Moss. *The Change Masters*. New York: Simon and Schuster, 1983. Full of insights and research on bringing about change from the middle of large organizations.

Kaye, Beverly. *Up Is Not the Only Way: A Guide for Career Development*. Englewood Cliffs, N.J.: Prentice-Hall, 1982. For readers interested in alternatives to climbing the corporate hierarchy. It also includes many good thoughts on career development. Kaye offers workshops.

Kirschenbaum, Howard. *Advanced Value Clarification*. La Jolla, California: University Associates, 1977. A good first source, and source of sources, on values.

Koontz, Harold, and Cyril O'Donnell. *Management*. New York: McGraw-Hill, 1976. Latest edition of the classic college text. Use it as you would a dictionary, for definitions of established theories and practices. Read the chapters on staff and service.

Levinson, Daniel J. *The Seasons of a Man's Life*. New York: Ballantine Books, 1978. Enlightening case studies of developmental patterns in men.

Maccoby, Michael. *The Leader*. New York: Simon and Schuster, 1981. Profiles of individuals with successful and unusual leadership styles.

McClelland, David C. *Power*. New York: Irvington Publishers, Inc., 1975. Many perspectives on power, especially McClelland's own. Research-based documentation of the importance of power in organizational life.

McLagan, Patricia, and Peter Krembs. *On the Level*. St. Paul, Minnesota: M & A Press, Inc., 1982. Very practical help on how to talk with your people about work. McLagan and Krembs offer related workshops.

Peck, M. Scott. *The Road Less Travelled*. New York: Simon and Schuster, 1978. For readers interested in values and spiritual growth as related to their work life.

Peters, Thomas J., and Robert H. Waterman, Jr. *In Search of Excellence*. New York: Harper & Row, 1982. The sucess of this book indicates our hunger for new management thought.

Peters, Thomas J., and Nancy Austin. *A Passion for Excellence*. New York: Random House, 1985. More stories and actions that show others making a leadership difference. A bit more "how to" than Peters's first book.

Tichy, Noel M. *Managing Strategic Change*. New York: John Wiley & Sons, 1983. Contains excellent thoughts and models dealing with all aspects of long-term change in large organizations.

Acknowledgements

After completing the second draft of this book, I decided it was time to consider who and what had helped me reach this point in my life and career. I was going to be the first person to write a book who actually acknowledged all of the people and organizations and institutions that had contributed significantly to the thoughts between two hard covers—even if it took pages, everyone would be mentioned.

Now I understand why there are so few names in most acknowledgments; it is simply an impossible task. There are friends, family, line executives, staff executives, external and internal consultants, clients, writers, associates, editors, researchers, presenters, subordinates, bosses, peers—chances are, if I know you and have worked with you, your ideas are related to some section of this book. For many of you, I can easily point out the section you influenced. Twenty years of staff work inside and outside of large organizations have left me indebted to many people.

There are some people who worked directly on the book with me, sorting and clarifying and dressing up my thoughts, whom I do want to mention. Ray Bard, book producer, shepherded me through the entire writing process and guided the book from conception through production. He was most important to my motivation. Leslie Stephens gave me early encouragement and critiqued a first draft. Alta Campbell accepted a difficult job when she agreed to work with the various drafts of the manuscript. Her ideas have been essential in bringing shape and order to my thoughts. Alison Tartt did the difficult job of copy editing. Eric Bellman entered changes and printed out numerous copies of numerous drafts. Sheila Kelly was invaluable help on the final draft. At home, she, Eric, Erin, and Tracy made working on this book easier by providing quiet support and giving me room to write.

My thanks to all of you.

THE AUTHOR

Geoff Bellman brings a wealth of experience to his writing. He spent fourteen years working in key staff positions in major corporations, two of them Fortune 500 companies. Since 1978 he has provided consultant services to a wide variety of clients through his firm GMB Associates, Ltd., formerly in Chicago, now located in Seattle, Washington.

While at G. D. Searle, AMOCO Corporation, and Ideal Basic Industries, Geoff's responsibilities ranged from personnel supervisor to vice-presidential assistant, from systems analyst to corporate director of development. The national and international clientele served through his consulting firm includes major corporations as well as small companies and governmental organizations.

Geoff is a regular contributor to journals such as *The Training and Development Journal, The Management Review,* and *Training*. He has a master's degree in business from the University of Oregon and is a member of the Organization Development Network, the American Society for Training and Development, and the Woodlands Group.